Kenneth R. Murray • M. R. Ha

Use of Force Training in Law Enforcement

A Reality Based Approach

 Springer

Kenneth R. Murray
Armiger Police Training Institute
Gotha, FL, USA

M. R. Haberfeld
City University of New York, John Jay
College of Criminal Justice
New York, NY, USA

ISSN 2192-8533   ISSN 2192-8541   (electronic)
SpringerBriefs in Criminology
ISSN 2194-6213   ISSN 2194-6221   (electronic)
SpringerBriefs in Policing
ISBN 978-3-030-59878-5   ISBN 978-3-030-59880-8   (eBook)
https://doi.org/10.1007/978-3-030-59880-8

This Springer imprint is published by the registered company Springer Nature Switzerland AG
The registered company address is: Gewerbestrasse 11, 6330 Cham, Switzerland

SpringerBriefs in Criminology

SpringerBriefs in Criminology present concise summaries of cutting edge research across the fields of Criminology and Criminal Justice. It publishes small but impactful volumes of between 50-125 pages, with a clearly defined focus. The series covers a broad range of Criminology research from experimental design and methods, to brief reports and regional studies, to policy-related applications.

The scope of the series spans the whole field of Criminology and Criminal Justice, with an aim to be on the leading edge and continue to advance research. The series will be international and cross-disciplinary, including a broad array of topics, including juvenile delinquency, policing, crime prevention, terrorism research, crime and place, quantitative methods, experimental research in criminology, research design and analysis, forensic science, crime prevention, victimology, criminal justice systems, psychology of law, and explanations for criminal behavior.

SpringerBriefs in Criminology will be of interest to a broad range of researchers and practitioners working in Criminology and Criminal Justice Research and in related academic fields such as Sociology, Psychology, Public Health, Economics and Political Science.

More information about this series at http://www.springer.com/series/10159

Dedicated to the memory of the fallen heroes of law enforcement.
K.R. Murray
M.R. Haberfeld

Acknowledgment

We would like to express our most profound gratitude to Judith Newlin, whose comments on this manuscript were invaluable to its final version.

Also, we would like to thank the Springer production team for their competence and professionalism.

Finally, we would like to thank Katie Chabalko for starting this project with us and her vision for its success.

Kenneth R. Murray
M. R. Haberfeld

Contents

1 Introduction 1
References 4

2 Introducing the Reality-Based Training: Blending Psychology, Philosophy, and Technology 7
The Reluctant Warrior 7
Overcoming Psychological Barriers 8
The Problem with Traditional Firearms Training 9
Unconscious Incompetence 10
Conscious Incompetence 10
Conscious Competence—CC 10
Unconscious Competence—UC 11
The Importance of Eye-Hand Coordination 14
Leg Two—Stress 14
Fear 15
References 16

3 Unrealistic Beliefs: When All Expectations Go Wrong—Talk, Fight, Shoot, or Leave? 17
Stress Recognition 17
Elevated Heart Rate 18
Visual Narrowing 19
Perceptual Distortion 19
Dominant Response Takes Over 20
Neurological Effects of Stress 21
Fighting 22
Posturing 23
References 23

4   Rules of Engagement: Addressing the "Unconsciously
Incompetent" Mode Through Scenario-Based Training   25
The Dichotomy of Previous Killing Experience.   26
Sensitivity Retraining   26
Rules of Engagement/Force Policy.   27
Justification to Use Lethal Force Versus the Necessity to Use
       Lethal Force   31
Spontaneous, Deliberate Lethal Force, and Reactive Lethal Force   33
Immediate Versus Imminent   34
Unclear Force Policies   35
Reactive.   37
Hesitation   38
References.   39

5   The Killing Experience: Unlikely Suspension of Judgment
and Time Out for Safety   41
Routine Experiences   42
Rarely Have to Go One-on-One for Very Long   43
Sterile Training   43
Negative Training Experiences   43
Negative Media Exposure   44
Training: Them   44
       Experience Is the Best Teacher   44
Training: Us   44
References.   47

6   The == of Reality-Based Training (RBT): The Delivery
of the "Unconscious Competence"   49
How Training Is Currently Done Versus a More Effective Way   50
Projectile-Based Training Considerations.   53
The Dangers of Projectile-Based Live Target Engagement   53
The Hodge-Podge of Doom   54
The Usefulness of Pain Penalties   54
The Usefulness of Marks During Live Target Engagement   56
The Necessity for Identical Equipment Manipulation   58
Learn to Accept and Channel the Effects of Stress.   59
Do Not Give It Away.   59
Stop "Killing" Your Students in Training   60
The Problem with Negative Reinforcement Training   62
Natural Conclusions to a Scenario   63
The Situation Is Under Control.   65
Suspect Is in Custody   65
The Suspect Has Been Shot   68

The Intervention Guidelines   68
The Intervention Points During a Scenario.   69
Unnatural Pause   69
Goofy Loop.   70
Meltdowns.   70
Physiological Meltdown   71
Psychological/Emotional Meltdown.   71
Caught Between a "Rock" and a Hard Place   72
Technological Meltdown.   73
The Intervention Questions.   74
Unnatural Conclusions to a Scenario   75
Safety Hazards   75
The Role Player Has Departed from the Script   75
References.   77

7   **A New Way of Thinking About Training**   79
Old Training Philosophy.   79
New Training Philosophy   80
The Building Blocks of Reality-Based Training.   81
Use Situations Your Officers Are Likely to Encounter   82
Catastrophic Events   83
Single Source Experience   83
Look for Patterns of Behavior in Your Agency's Case Files.   83
Change Endings to Avoid Programmed Responses   84
If Your Standard Is Perfection, Your Students Will Be Excellent   84
Unsafe Training Practices Tend to Magnify Themselves in the Real
      World   85
Observe and Correct All Unsafe Behavior   85
Reality-Based Training Will Bring to Light Issues for Clarification
      by the Agency   86
Tidying Up Sloppy Departmental Policy   86
Play "What If?" in Training and Fix the Problems Before They
      Occur in Real Situations   87
Professionals Have Pre-conditioned Responses to Stressful Events.   88
Make Training Realistic   88
Use Realistic Props and Training Versions of Equipment   89
Role Player Props   90
Use Realistic Settings   90
Use Realistic Situations   92
Teach from the Simple to the Complex to Ensure Competency   93
Reality-Based Training Requires Judgment and Teaches
      Situational Awareness   95
References.   96

8   Conclusion and Final Thoughts.   97
    Debrief, Remediation, and After Action Review   97
    Scenario.   98
    Debriefing   98
    Immediate Remediation   100
    After Action Review   100
    Final Thoughts   101
    References.   102

Index.   105

Chapter 1
Introduction

This book draws broadly on a comprehensive teaching manual developed by one of the co-authors Kenneth R. Murray and was supplemented by the academic insights from the second co-author Dr. Maria (Maki) Haberfeld. It provides a combination of the academic background for understanding why and how the police use force, especially deadly force, and how their actions can be improved through the Reality-Based Training (RBT), a concept that can save their lives and the lives of those they are sworn to serve and protect. Throughout this book, the reader will learn how creative approaches to training can assist law enforcement personnel in acquiring, developing, and enhancing skills associated with the use of physical force necessary to accomplish compliance.

The twenty-first-century public's demands and expectations of the criminal justice system are contradictory. People demand a lot but often have low expectations of law enforcement.

In the 1980s, demands escalated as sharp increases in violent crime led the public to support spending more money on local policing efforts. Police chiefs responded by experimenting with varying approaches, settling (for now) on "Community-Oriented Policing" as the "modern" approach to effective policing (Haberfeld 2002; Kimbrough 2016; Leventakis and Haberfeld 2018a, b, 2019).

Fast forward almost three decades and the expected changes did not take place, and the rift between the public and its police forces seems to be more serious than ever before (Haberfeld 2018).

Nothing exemplifies better the complicated nature of police-community relations than the quote from the legendary August Vollmer, Chief of Police of Berkley, California:

> The citizen expects police officers to have the wisdom of Solomon, the courage of David, the strength of Samson, the patience of Job, the leadership of Moses, the kindness of the Good Samaritan, the strategical training of Alexander, the faith of Daniel, the diplomacy of Lincoln, the tolerance of the Carpenter of Nazareth, and finally, an intimate knowledge of

© The Author(s), under exclusive licence to Springer Nature Switzerland AG 2021
K. R. Murray, M. R. Haberfeld, *Use of Force Training in Law Enforcement*,
SpringerBriefs in Criminology, https://doi.org/10.1007/978-3-030-59880-8_1

every branch of the natural, biological, and social sciences. If he had all these, he might be a good policeman! (Bain 1939)

It appears that the more civilized we become as a society the more we resent the notion of the organization, which is authorized to solve society's problems through the use of coearcive force. However, when things become really bad, we noticed how quickly many people were willing to sacrifice various measures of personal freedom in the wake of the events of September 11, 2001. When the wolf is at the door, those who are unprepared to defend themselves are quick to call for help from those who would face the danger in their stead.

The question becomes, when does freedom find itself at direct odds with safety? Society accepts that the all-important Freedom of Speech can be restricted in the interest of public safety. It is illegal to arbitrarily stand in a crowded theater and shout "fire!" This type of restriction is acceptable to the masses because there is nothing "politically incorrect" about it. The concept of "profiling," on the other hand, is shunned by lawmakers because of the negative attention it has received in the wake of legal action taken by civil rights activists over the years, past and present, examined in the harshest light.

Much of the problem stems from the unrealistic image that the protected have of the protectors, painted largely by the media through television and movies. Very few lawmen or soldiers are stone killers. They are not all masters of the martial arts. They are not machines that can easily switch from guidance counselor to executioner in the blink of an eye. Taking the life of another human being is an unnatural act for all human beings. It is a learned behavior that goes against our genetic coding. In fact, the preservation of human life is one of the strongest urges of the human spirit, so strong that the noble will sacrifice their own lives in the defense of the helpless, and so important that the principle of Reasonable Doubt guarding against accidental execution of an innocent man is based on the eighteenth century precept of William Blackstone, who said:

"It is better that ten guilty persons escape than one innocent suffer." (https://www.oxfor-dreference.com/view/10.1093/acref/9780191826719.001.0001/q-oro-ed4-00006117)

This sets the bar rather high for the modern police officer. And the expectations of society are so exacting that even in the mayhem of a life and death confrontation, an officer is expected to make lightning fast decisions. God help the officer who makes the wrong decision, and yet God will surely meet the officer who hesitates while trying to navigate through the maelstrom of uncertainty that often accompanies a lethal force encounter, only to be bested by an opponent who has prepared in advance for a lethal encounter through his/her own pre-conditioning to take a life.

This pre-conditioning that many of society's high-level offenders have received comes from their experiences in the "mean streets," be it gang affiliation, crime ridden neighborhods, and exposure to violent street encounters in general. Conversely, today's police officer is typically the product of a completely opposite social environment. An officer's level of socialization can actually hamper him/her to the extent that it is often a paralyzing impediment during a life-threatening encounter.

As a means of overcoming such a handicap, Reality-Based Training can assist police personnel in understanding their duty to use lethal force when and where necessary. It can provide the crucial conditioning and stress inoculations needed by officers if they are to become psychologically equipped to deliver lethal force when required, in situations where an unprepared individual would otherwise face catastrophic consequences.

Before we can effectively study the art and science of Reality-Based Training that often simulates the taking of human life, it is necessary to have a thorough understanding of the underlying architecture of the human psyche as it pertains to killing another person, since this is the area of the psyche that we are attempting to rewire.

Until we were provided a clearer understanding of the various "human" factors associated with a gunfight by David Grossman in his book *On Killing* (1995), trainers had been quick to blame the majority of poor performance on high-stress levels or poor shooting skills. We now know that hit ratios in gunfights do not improve simply by focusing training efforts on reducing stress and improving shooting skill. Further, any attempt to develop a simulation-training program without incorporating a solid understanding of the underlying psychology governing the use of lethal force is not likely to produce the desired outcomes.

Before we can overcome the psychological factors that might impede an officer's performance in a gunfight, we have to determine the extent these factors are present in each officer. One of the true benefits of Reality-Based Training is that the innate psychological safeguards and barriers which might be present in each officer that contribute to his/her reluctance to taking another life can be measured, *if the training is sufficiently realistic and properly structured.*

In 2020, it is of critical importance for police forces around the country, and around the world for that matter, to understand that given the proliferation of police-citizen encounters's images, compliments of the abundance of various electronic devices present and recording the encounters, be it the smartphones and cameras used by the public or the body worn cameras (BWC), there is much less room for the proverbial "errors of judgment." According to Ariel et al. (2016b), the two main principles of body worn cameras are to: (1) reduce use-of-force incidents by police, and (2) reduce citizen-complaints against police. It is highly plausible that a reduction in use-of-force incidents and citizen-complaints against police would be beneficial to most municipalities for community relations and to possibly reduce monetary expenditures associated with litigations. The use of body cameras can also create an aura of transparency with the public, demonstrating that law enforcement has nothing to hide by exhibiting recorded incidents where suspicion of abuse is alleged or perceived. Police BWC use has been expanding across the United States, and in 2015, the U.S. Department of Justice awarded over $23 million in funding to support programs for BWCs. Some 95% of large police departments have either implemented the program or anticipate its use (Yokum et al. 2017).

Although it may not be a panacea for all issues related to policing, the use of body cameras is viewed as an effective tool to decrease the need for officers to use force and reduce the number of complaints made against police by citizens (Miller and Toliver 2014).

However, some more recent research findings on the impact of BWC on the use of force by the police generated mixed findings (Ariel et al. 2016a, 2017). Furthermore, although some encouraging results were found in a number of police departments in the United States, like in Rialto, California, Las Vegas, Nevada, Boston, Massachusetts and Spokane, Washington, research conducted in London, UK and Washington D.C. was not as convincing. These inconsistencies were verified in a 2019 study which examined a compilation of 70 empirical BWC studies and found no statistically significant or consistent results related to civilizing behavior in police-citizen encounters (Lum et al. 2019).

Regardless of what the research is showing, given the calls for more accountability on the part of police departments when use of force is deployed to achieve compliance and the resistance of police departments to the changes in their standard operating procedures (Brown et al. (2020) 7/24/2020), it is clear that realistic and properly structured training is not just long overdue but simply a necessary and mandatory component of our future police forces. This book will provide the much-needed template to achieve the goal of effective use of force and minimize the number of complaints and accusations from the public. It is our hope that police academies around the country, and the world, will find it useful and effective in rethinking some of the aspects of their training components.

References

Ariel, B., Sutherland, A., Henstock, D., Young, J., Drover, P., Sykes, J., & Henderson, R. (2016a). Report: Increases in police use of force in the presence of body-worn cameras are driven by officer discretion: A protocol-based subgroup analysis of ten randomized experiments. *Journal of Experimental Criminology, 12(3), 453–463*.

Ariel, B., Sutherland, A., Henstock, D., Young, J., Drover, P., Sykes, J., & Henderson, R. (2016b). Wearing body cameras increases assaults against officers and does not reduce police use of force: Results from a global multi-site experiment. *European Journal of Criminology, 13(6), 744–755*.

Ariel, B., Sutherland, A., Henstock, D., Young, J., & Sosinski, G. (2017). The deterrence spectrum: Explaining why police body-worn cameras 'work' or 'backfire' in aggressive police–public encounters. *Policing: A Journal of Policy and Practice, 12(1), 6–26*.

Bain, R. (1939). The Policeman on the Beat. *Science Monthly, 48*, 5.

Brown, R. S., Parascandola, R., & Annese, J. (2020). Cop big: DAs won't charge choke cases. *New York Daily News*, Retrieved on July 24, 2020, http://enewspaper.nydailynews.com/infinity/article_share.aspx?guid=a300273b-727d-40e2-8f82-26b903c4dac8

Grossman, D. (1995). *On killing: The psychological cost of learning to kill in war and society*. Boston: Little Brown.

Haberfeld, M. R. (2002). Journal of Policing: An International Journal of Police Strategies and Management, 25(1) Guest Editor of the Issue: *Community Policing: An International Perspective*

Haberfeld, M. R. (2018). *Critical Issues in Police Training*. Pearson Customs Publishing. Retrieved on July 23, 2020, https://www.oxfordreference.com/view/10.1093/acref/9780191826719.001.0001/q-oro-ed4-00006117

Kimbrough, C. (2016). Building bridges: Community policing for the 21st century. *National Civic Review, 105*(4), 3–13.

Leventakis, G., & Haberfeld, M. R. (Eds.). (2018a). *Societal implications of community oriented policing and technology* (Briefs in Policing Series). New York: Springer.

Leventakis, G., & Haberfeld, M. R. (Eds.). (2018b). *Community oriented policing and technological innovations* (Briefs in Policing Series). New York: Springer.

Leventakis, G., & Haberfeld, M. R. (Eds.). (2019). *Synergy of community policing and technology: A comparative approach* (Briefs in Policing Series). New York: Springer.

Lum, C., Stoltz, M., Koper, C. S., & Scherer, J. A. (2019). Research on body-worn cameras: What we know, what we need to know. *Criminology & Public Policy., 18*, 93–118. https://doi.org/10.1111/1745-9133.12412.

Miller, L., Toliver, J., & Police Executive Research Forum. (2014). *Implementing a Body-Worn camera program: Recommendations and lessons learned*. Washington, DC: Office of Community Oriented Policing Services.

Yokum, D., Ravishankar, A., & Coppock, A. (2017). *Evaluating the effects of police body-worn cameras: A randomized controlled trial* (pp. 1–27). Washington, DC: The Lab @ DC, Office of the City Administrator, Executive Office of the Mayor.

Chapter 2
Introducing the Reality-Based Training: Blending Psychology, Philosophy, and Technology

The Reluctant Warrior

As we look closer at the human aspects of lethal force encounters, we discover that some of the hesitation to decisively engage a lethal threat by many officers can be attributed to societal pre-conditioning and unrealistic expectations that many of the new officers bring to the job. Lt. James Como (2010), a commander with the Ocoee, FL Police Department and has nearly 20 years as instructor in the martial arts, describes a phenomenon he refers to as "The Reluctant Warrior."

Many of today's police applicants begin their quest for a law enforcement position with very altruistic motivations. To "Protect and Serve" sums up their view of what a police officer is, and is expected to be. This outlook is further reinforced and encouraged in the classroom settings at the police academy. While not realizing, or perhaps not wanting to admit it, many police officers fall into the category of the Reluctant Warrior. Society wants the "kinder, gentler" protector-guardian, and this influences to a great degree the types of training law enforcement personnel "need" or "should" receive to achieve this end. Quick life and death decisions made by law enforcement officers often meet with criticism and second-guesses, with the ultimate punishment by way of a lawsuit.

Law enforcement is one of the few professions in which training needs are often dictated, shaped, and sometimes forced by ill-informed public opinion and outcry. But quite often, we get no better treatment from "our own" in the law enforcement community. It will oftentimes take a tragedy to motivate upper echelon management to order an inquiry for the evaluation of training methods and program effectiveness. Internal administrative pressure, the looming specter of a lawsuit, and lack of understanding coupled with unrealistic expectations from society further contribute to an officer's sense of reluctance and hesitation when rightfully called upon to resolve a violent encounter. This hesitation too often results in officer injury— or worse.

© The Author(s), under exclusive licence to Springer Nature Switzerland AG 2021
K. R. Murray, M. R. Haberfeld, *Use of Force Training in Law Enforcement*,
SpringerBriefs in Criminology, https://doi.org/10.1007/978-3-030-59880-8_2

With many firearms and physical training modules quite lacking to begin with, effectively equipping officers to adequately defend themselves and others becomes an arduous task. The overemphasis focus on interpersonal communication skills and sensitivity training separate from that of the reality-based firearms/physical training system has the unintended, adverse effect of almost banishing the officer's need to use force and, sometimes, deadly force.

Many martial artists and marksmen have found out, to their dismay, that merely practicing a technique or drill over and over again, while ignoring the psychological aspects of combat, most often had the opposite result of what the intense training was meant to instill. Unlike the committed martial artist or soldier, the average police officer does not spend much time practicing the physical skills learned in departmental training, much less the emotional and psychological conditioning exercises needed to mentally place one "in the zone" when necessary.

In addition to the way we train, denial, laziness, threat of law suits, and unrealistic societal expectations could probably all be faulted for the increased inability of officers to accomplish the mission set before them. Self-discipline and self-mastery have seemingly gone by the wayside in lieu of the quick fix, an ultimate catchall technique that can be learned and mastered in an hour, and retained with little to no supplemental training. With expandable batons giving way to chemical agents, only to be replaced by TASER®s, law enforcement officers are forever being told that their answer to violent conflict management will be found in a tool or the latest gadget, that once mastered, will solve most if not all their problems. These tools are rarely incorporated into a reality-based comprehensive training system, but rather are taught as distinct unto themselves. This sets the officer up for improper threat assessment and poor use-of-force transition. Someone who is truly concerned with being tactical will practice transitional techniques. These should "flow" and officers should be capable of transition, both in escalation and de-escalation. Contrary to belief by some, law enforcement officers are expected to de-escalate their response when the level of threat diminishes. They should also have a general idea of when a tactic is not accomplishing its intended objective, and how to transition into another, more effective one.

It would be easy to dismiss the above officer responses as anomalies, bad examples, or isolated instances of poor tactics, but the problem is so frighteningly pervasive that virtually no one is immune to performing in a similar fashion. Many situations similar to the above involve officers who functioned as instructors within their agency for those same areas of practice in which things went wrong.

Overcoming Psychological Barriers

The first step in figuring a way past the psychological barriers to effective and decisive action is through definition of the problem, which seems to be a three-headed monster. Most of the situations in law enforcement that lead to costly resolutions by way of lawsuits or injuries can be cataloged into three major groups:

1. Officers refusing to use lethal force when both justified and necessary
2. Officers using inadequate lower levels of force when higher levels are both justified and necessary
3. Officers using excessive force

The trainings that agencies are providing to their officers allegedly address these three areas of concern, yet the problems regularly persist. This raises the question of the adequacy of the current training methods. Ostensibly, if officers were provided adequate training in these areas, the problems would not be so pervasive.

Many agencies tend to place the blame for poor performance over two of the following elements Skill and Stress, in situations where officers have performed in a less than textbook manner. Until recently, these were the only two factors which were used to explain critical failures.

Even today, when an officer responds poorly either in training or on the street, we are quick to prescribe more training to improve skills, or various techniques to reduce the stress, and often ignore the human factors. Consequently, training programs and training simulation technologies have directed much of their focus toward improving the technical expertise of the trainees. Unfortunately, these improvements in training techniques and technologies did not really change the overall success in terms of improving performance during critical incidents.

An officer could be the most proficient marksman on the planet, yet would most probably be useless in a gunfight if his personal beliefs interfered with the taking of a human life. In such an instance, it is the marksman's psychology that requires the most work, yet the effective programming of an officer's survival psychology is the area that is short-changed because survival mindset theory is usually taught as an academic topic rather than through practical exercises. Beyond that, many administrators are quite timid about publicly acknowledging that the possibility of killing people is in fact a part of the job description of their officers.

.

The Problem with Traditional Firearms Training

Much of the firearms training that has occurred in law enforcement and military circles was designed around a scoring system intended to simply "qualify" a participant. Qualification merely demonstrates the ability to put a certain number of holes in a target from varying distances, inside a predetermined time, within a controlled environment.

When developing any skill there are four levels of integration during its acquisition. There is a well-established principle governing the progressive nature of skill mastery. This hierarchy is:

- Unconscious Incompetence
- Conscious Incompetence
- Conscious Competence

- Unconscious Competence

Grinder and colleagues are the developers of NLP (Neuro-Linguistic Programming). Grinder's hierarchy actually included a fifth level which was the "Conscious Competence of Unconscious Competence" or the expert level at which trainers are able to understand and to teach or train others in a skill Grinder and Bandler (1981); Grinder and Pucelik (2012).

Unconscious Incompetence

To understand the concept of Unconscious Incompetence, imagine heading out to Anygunrange, USA on a weekend and watching the collection of modern day gun-fighters blazing away with their huge hand-cannons at a target placed ten feet away. They will pull back the target and gaze upon their handiwork with the pride of a new father examining his first-born son. The point here is that anyone can shoot. Pick up a loaded firearm, press the trigger and voilà ... you are shooting. Shooting accurately is another story.

Conscious Incompetence

To begin to learn to shoot accurately, our shooting enthusiast must be informed that there is a set of sights on the firearm and taught to align them with the target. They can also be educated about grip, stance, trigger control, breathing, follow-through, and all the other minute details associated with precision marksmanship. With all this new information, he/she becomes Consciously Incompetent, that is, he/she is now aware of important small details that he/she never even knew were important. Although he/she is not yet able to reliably perform well, he/she now knows how to shoot well, and it will take some practice with these skills to gain proficiency.

Conscious Competence—CC

After training, practice, and repetition, he/she can shoot well if he/she pays attention to all the necessary fine motor skills he/she has just learned. As he/she becomes more technically proficient, he/she can begin to add additional complexities such as time constraints, target movement, target discrimination, etc. When his/her shot groups start to widen out again, he/she must redirect his attention to the various components of precision shooting, such as sight alignment and trigger control. Once again, he/she will begin to tighten up his/her groups. He/she has now reached the level of Conscious Competence or CC.

CC is the level that most people can easily achieve in any skill through training, practice, and repetition. Interval training will ensure that those skills do not completely deteriorate, since most skills have a "shelf life" if not practiced. Unfortunately, CC is the level at which most law enforcement and military personnel stop training with their firearms and defensive tactics. CC is the level at which they can demonstrate a base level of proficiency one to four times a year ... on a range or in a gym ... under ideal conditions. They have qualified. The regulatory agency tasked with overseeing their proficiency has checked a box for liability purposes.

Unfortunately for most military and law enforcement personnel, physical fights and armed engagements occur in less than ideal conditions. Lighting is poor, information is imperfect, threats are dynamic, situations are deteriorating quickly, blood chemistry is rapidly changing, and human physiology is priming itself for the fight of its life.

Most officers do not make a personal commitment to firearms practice, in fact many detest guns, never mind taking pride in carrying one. And while there is a mandate within the law enforcement and military communities to ensure a base level of firearms proficiency for those who must carry weapons, most agencies do not have the time and financial resources to provide officers with the firearms training time or ammunition necessary to condition shooting skills to the level necessary to perform predictably well in a gunfight.

Even those who train to an exceptionally high level of proficiency must go a step further if they are to have reliable access to those skills in a situation where the threat is dynamic. Tony Blauer relates a training situation that highlights this reality.

Unconscious Competence—UC

UC is the level of proficiency where optimum performance of a motor skill can be delivered without the need for conscious resources being allocated to it. An example of UC that most people over the age of 21 can relate to is driving a car. Most drivers with several years of experience can start their car in the driveway in the morning, drive to work, and have little recollection of the journey.

Driving a car is an extremely complex motor skill requiring millions of mental calculations and physiological adjustments necessary to safely navigate the route and eventually park the car at the final destination. Any threat cues such as traffic lights, school crossings, or erratic drivers, are immediately processed by the subconscious mind and effective counter-measures are implemented without the need for conscious intervention. The conscious mind is free to make higher-level decisions dealing with the relative importance and final disposition of those threat cues.

One difficulty in the allocation of conscious resources is the limitations imposed by our human capacity for conscious thought. According to Miller (1956), the average human can keep seven, plus or minus two, "chunks" of information in his/her conscious awareness during non-stressful conditions. That is one reason why seven-digit phone numbers are much easier to remember than ten digits. Have you ever had someone give you a telephone number without "chunking" it? 4075327380 is a lot harder to remember than 407 .... 532 .... 7380 because we have been conditioned to "chunk" phone numbers into the 3-3-4 pattern.

For larger groups of information to be memorized, it is necessary to organize that information. Miller demonstrates how "chunking" works using the following example – look at the following string of letters for two seconds then close the book and write down as many as you can remember in order:

ITTIBMCBSATTTWANBC

How many did you get?

Now let us break the string up into some easy-to-remember "chunks" and try again.

ITT   IBM   CBS   ATT   TWA   NBC

If you cheated by reading ahead, try this on anybody who has not read this book, and I think I can guarantee that once people "chunk" the information down, they can remember it better. In fact right now you can probably close your eyes and remember most if not all of the three-letter groups, yet would be hard pressed to write out the original letter sequence.

Physiological or "muscle memory" works much the same way and this identical principle can be observed during firearms proficiency practice with an unskilled shooter. Until all the various motor skills are "chunked" into a single piece of motor memory, the mind and body treat everything individually. When he/she is focused on his/her front sight and trigger control, he/she does not pay attention to follow-through. Focus his/her attention on grip and breathing, and he/she forgets to look for his/her front sight.

When building the skills necessary for using a gun in a real life situation, the chunking of motor skills can be compared with building language skills. Think of this type of skill building in terms of "creating a survival sentence." Learning the "language of survival" is similar to learning to speak a foreign language. Each individual skill is like a letter in a word. The word "DRAW" for instance includes various individual mini-tasks (letters) necessary to disengage any retention features of the holster, achieve a proper grip on the pistol, presentation of the pistol, etc. Failure of any one of these small skills will result in the unsuccessful completion of the word "DRAW."

The "Survival Sentence" is made up of a number of "words" such as "THREAT RECOGNITION," "DRAW," "COVER," "COMMUNICATE," "MOVEMENT," "SHOOT," etc. Any failure to complete any of the "words" in the survival "sentence" may lead to failure at some level. Not recognizing a threat is a big problem. Not being able to get a pistol out and functioning is a big problem. Not utilizing cover is a big problem. Failure to communicate to the suspect, a partner, or dispatch is a big problem. Lack of movement is a big problem. Ideally, each "word" in the "Survival Sentence" must be thoroughly learned and integrated at the Unconscious

Competence level so that in the context of a life-threatening encounter, the "Survival Sentence" is part of the "native language."

In fact once the skill of tactical shooting becomes integrated at the Unconscious Competence level, the survival sentence becomes a single, representative survival "thought" where all the "words" in that "sentence" become "chunked" into a single representative "word:" "ENGAGE." All the skills then needed to engage that threat reside as a single chunk of motor memory, and the conscious mind is freed to deal with other complexities that might arise. This is the power of "chunking." Unfortunately, because individuals are not taking it upon themselves to learn each "word" and practice the "sentence" until it becomes second nature, they find themselves fumbling with a phrase book at a critical juncture. Their survival sentence is incomplete and fragmented.

Kosslyn and Koenig (1995) describe how the brain processes various events and how the body initiates action to those events in their book, *Wet Mind - The New Cognitive Neuroscience*. There is an entire page in the book full of boxes and arrows detailing the systems, sub-systems, and sub-subsystems in an effort to provide some insight into the complexity of the neural processes dealing with thought and action. The effective functioning of these subsystems for officer safety purposes presupposes that adequate previous learning has occurred, storing them as a "chunk" of motor memory that Kosslyn and Koenig refer to as a "torque profile." Without the skill building, each individual component of the desired movements will require conscious intervention. This is the value of repetition for skill building—so that a desired movement such as drawing a gun and accurately lining it up with the target becomes a single chunk, or torque profile.

Kosslyn and Koening refer to the concepts of "the target" and "via points" with relation to an automatic response. These scientific terms indicate how information connecting a threat stimulus to a proper response is stored; it does not refer to the target being shot at. Once a person has stored the torque profile through sufficient practice, the conscious mind will be free to make a target selection and give the order to shoot while all the complex motor skills combine in symphony to carry out that order. As with any other complex skill, however, it depreciates if not continually practiced. Because tactical shooting is an intricate system of motor movements, there are no shortcuts to doing well.

Despite the fact that we live in an instant gratification society, there is no shortcut to shooting well. Because of the dedication of time necessary for practice to become proficient, well-intentioned firearms trainers and gun writers keep searching for that illusive shortcut; some simpler training methodology; some new stance or grip that will allow officers to simply decide to shoot and have the weapon magically fire itself with a high degree of precision.

The Importance of Eye-Hand Coordination

Regardless of how you stand, if you do not practice lining up your weapon with the target and fire a lot of ammunition to confirm that alignment (or use some form of simulator that aids in that confirmation), accurate fire will for the most part be attributable to luck.

The human body is extremely capable of quickly learning how to perform eye-hand coordination skills. Humans complete every manipulative task based on this ability. We do not answer phones or scratch our noses without engaging the operating system in charge of eye-hand coordination, and we are capable of amazing feats once conscious resources are directed toward programming it to achieve specific results. A trained eye can break down rapidly occurring events to the extent that professional baseball players can track a ninety-mile per hour change up pitch, swing a bat, adjust the position of that bat during the swing, time the swing to hit the ball at the exact moment it exists in a certain place in space, and occasionally direct the ball where they want it to go. Compared with the complexities of hitting a baseball, accurate shooting is easy. Both are eye-hand coordination skills. The big difference lies in the training philosophies of the participants..

Given the time and financial limitations faced by agencies, integrating the complex motor skills associated with accurate shooting will ultimately rest with a level of personal commitment on the part of the individual officer. Fifteen minutes a day of dry practice (under safe and controlled conditions of course) will make an immense difference in the ability to deliver highly accurate fire during a life-threatening encounter. Fifteen minutes a week would easily make the difference in terms of weapon presentation, sight alignment, and trigger control. A firearms instructor can only do so much to help someone improve his/her skills. It is up to the student to do the training. A strength coach can teach you the exercises necessary to make your muscles bigger and can observe you to ensure correct form, but he cannot lift the weight for you. If the student does not do the work, the result (or actually lack of results) is predictable.

It is a safe bet to say that purely from the Skill perspective, law enforcement personnel are nowhere near the level of proficiency that will ensure success in a close combat gun battle or life-threatening physical confrontation.

Leg Two—Stress

Siddle (1995) teaches us about the many physiological changes that may degrade your ability to react effectively if your sympathetic nervous system turns on the hormone tap, dumping its survival soup into the bloodstream. But as mentioned in the previous section, activation of the sympathetic nervous system is fundamentally connected to individual perception of the level of threat faced by an officer. If an officer is aware of his/her surroundings and the situation so as not to be taken by surprise, has the advantages of time, distance, cover, and has confidence in his/her abilities, it is possible that the sympathetic nervous system may not be activated to the point where it becomes counterproductive to optimal performance. The officer will then often have the ability to respond with controlled aggression to a life-threatening problem.

The response to a life-threatening encounter by someone properly conditioned to the event is often one of exhilaration and controlled aggression. Tony Blauer (1983) has dedicated much of his life's work as a defensive tactics instructor, teaching people how to engage after a "flinch response" has happened. Blauer's S.P.E.A.R. SYSTEM techniques are designed to condition participants how to convert the primal "startle-flinch" response into effective action by building an experiential bridge to whichever defensive tactics techniques they are already using. His unique system and training exercises provide an extremely effective response to surprise attacks, which will go a long way toward maintaining or regaining control in a crisis or after a surprise attack. Losing control is undesirable since it limits access to otherwise normally available mental and physical resources.

Fear

Degradation of "the personality" is often directly connected to the way a person responds to a stressful stimulus. *Sharpening the Warrior's Edge* does a good job of enlightening us as to what physical manifestations might be expected during a stressful incident if the mind interprets a situation as "fearful." But what is fear?

What many refer to as "fear" is actually "anxiety." Fear is a mobilizing instinct. Anxiety, on the other hand, is a paralyzing state of the emotions, rooted mainly in perception. At some level of cognition, the mind makes judgments about all the situations in our lives, and during stress-producing incidents it will determine what will or will not be processed as fearful, whether or not that determination is even rational. It is all about perceived danger and not necessarily actual danger. Why is it that a skydiver can stand on the tailgate of an airplane, analyze the ground 14,000 feet below, and when he/she reaches the right spot, can jump out of that airplane without so much as a second thought in the name of entertainment, yet some people cannot even imagine being in an airplane without breaking out in a cold sweat?

To use a simplistic explanation, fright and exhilaration begin as virtually identical emotions, producing similar physiological responses until the mind intervenes. The mind will make a judgment about the experience, usually based upon the outcome of past experiences, and this in turn generates the emotion. Based on that judgment, an unconscious decision will be made as to how it wants the body to behave. If the decision is that the experience is "fun," the adrenaline rush adds to the enjoyment. If the decision is that the experience is "frightening," then the sympathetic nervous system kicks in, dumping well over a hundred different chemicals into the bloodstream to mobilize the body for survival. This is when skills practiced to merely the Conscious Competence level begin to deteriorate, or possibly fail altogether.

References

Blauer, T. (1983). Effective self-defense. *Inside Kung-Fu August*, 85–87.

Como, J. (2010). *Commander with the Ocoee*, FL Police Department. Personal communication.

Grinder, J., & Bandler, R. (1981). *Trance-formations*. Moab: Real People Press.

Grinder, J., & Pucelik, F. (2012). *The origins of neuro linguistic programming*. Carmarthen: Crown House Publishing.

Kosslyn, S. M., & Koenig, O. (1995). *Wet mind: The new cognitive neuroscience*. New York: Free Press.

Miller, G. A. (1956). The magic number seven plus or minus two: Some limits on our capacity for processing information. *Psychological Review, 63*, 91–97.

Siddle, B. K. (1995). *Sharpening the warrior's edge*. Millstadt: PPCT Research Publications.

Chapter 3
Unrealistic Beliefs: When All Expectations Go Wrong—Talk, Fight, Shoot, or Leave?

Unrealistic beliefs can take a psychological or emotional toll. For instance, if an officer has the expectation that a suspect will immediately cease his/her hostile actions when hit by fists, spray, impact weapons, TASER®s, or bullets, he/she is in for a rude awakening when fighting an opponent who continues to fight well beyond the point that he/she should have been brought down. Having a false sense of security based on ineffective defensive tactics can also shatter the psyche of an officer who mistakenly believes that this or that "move" will bring about a swift conclusion to an encounter. Such misconceptions can have a chilling effect on an unprepared officer.

Stress Recognition

It is important, then, to be able to recognize and identify the things that might occur during stressful encounters if they are to be used to one's advantage (Klinger 2004). Generally, some of the physical and mental responses to acute stress that will have a direct impact on an officer's ability to effectively respond to the situation are:

- Elevated heart rate
- Hormones get dumped into the bloodstream
- Visual narrowing
- Perceptual distortion
- Dominant responses take over

According to Haberfeld (2018), Critical Stress Incident can be generated by any situation or encounter with a citizen, peer, organization, or others, from which a police officer emerges with a feeling or perception that "justice has not been served" for him and/or the others. This approach further amplifies the need to understand the various aspects of stress in police training of use of force.

© The Author(s), under exclusive licence to Springer Nature Switzerland AG 2021   17
K. R. Murray, M. R. Haberfeld, *Use of Force Training in Law Enforcement*,
SpringerBriefs in Criminology, https://doi.org/10.1007/978-3-030-59880-8_3

Elevated Heart Rate

Siddle (1995), one of the early law enforcement researchers into the physiology of stress during life-threatening encounters, hypothesized a connection between heart rate and skill performance. He/she represented this relationship graphically using the Inverted "U" Hypothesis. According to this hypothesis, as the heart rate rises in response to a threat stimulus, varying degrees of skills become inaccessible. Siddle suggests that fine motor skills begin to quickly deteriorate beyond 115 b.p.m. and complex motor skills become nearly inaccessible beyond 175 b.p.m. He/she further states that an elevated heart rate can happen very quickly, with the heart rate elevating from a resting rate of 60–80 b.p.m., to over 200 beats per minute in under a second.

According to Vonk (2004), in a scenario with little or no physical requirements, it seems as though the lower the heart rate the better the performance. She also questions whether there is a universal "inverted U" with specific numbered parameters outlying the "optimal performance zone," as Siddle has suggested. Building on Siddle's work on heart rate, Vonk postulates that it seems to make more sense that each person's "optimal performance zone" would be unique to that particular individual based on a multitude of factors, and may not necessarily lie between 115 and 145 b.p.m.

Vonk claims that when attempting to study heart rate during critical encounters, the equipment used in data collection is paramount. The use of high-resolution heart rate measuring equipment, like the Polar S810 is significant because all other monitors, including the one used in the Survival Scores Research Project by FLETC, record a five second average instead of recording every single heart beat.

In an attempt to teach officers to fight through the effects of an elevated heart rate, some trainers have tried to replicate these effects by having officers perform physical exertion exercises before fighting or shooting. Although this is well-intentioned, it is by and large misleading. It has been discovered that although there would be some effect on shooting or fighting performance from shortness of breath and shaky muscles, the difference in blood chemistry is markedly different between individuals who have an elevated heart rate as a result of exercise and those whose rate is up due to a hormonal (stress-induced) response. More particularly, there is a vast physiological difference between fear and exertion.

While more research is required to determine whether there is a direct causative relationship between the heart rate and physiological impairments, it seems useful to use the heart rate as one of the important measuring sticks of physiological arousal (when the heart rate is up as a result of a fear response, rather than through exertion). Whether an elevated heart rate is the cause of many of the physiological impairments that are experienced during survival stress, using techniques such as patterned breathing and positive self-talk to lower the heart rate seem to have the systemic effect of reducing the other negative symptoms associated with a stressful incident.

According to Kureczka (1996) who studied extensively traumatic events during various critical encounters and their impact on individual behaviors, the definition of a critical incident and its influences must remain fluid because what affects one officer might not affect another.

Visual Narrowing

One of the common experiences of officers in a life-threatening encounter is some measure of narrowing of the field of visual information. In an effort to teach students to overcome the effects of visual narrowing, firearms trainers will often use the common range command "scan and breathe." Telling students in a range setting to do this will usually achieve the result of having the shooters insignificantly nodding their heads back and forth. It is important to get students to truly understand why they are doing this so that it has relevance if there is ever a need. Scanning is necessary to actually see threats that may exist outside their reduced field of vision. Breathing, systematic and patterned breathing, will have the effect of lowering the heart rate, supplying more oxygen to the brain, and reducing the level of anxiety, which can lead to a higher level of cognitive clarity.

Siddle (1995) suggests that under high stress, our visual system becomes one of the casualties, resulting in a reduction in peripheral vision as well as the inability to focus on the front sight of a weapon.

Perceptual Distortion

Other effects such as auditory occlusion can be sufficiently severe that gunshots may not be heard or registered in the conscious mind. Neither will shouted warnings, nor radio transmissions. Other awareness limitations include the possibility of an officer to be unaware of being hurt, even if they have been shot or stabbed, because of a temporary suppression of pain awareness.

The perception of time compression and expansion often occurs, and events may be remembered out of sequence or remembered incorrectly, if remembered at all. According to research done by leading edge police psychologists Artwohl and Christensen (1997) there have also been extensive reports of officers vividly remembering things that never even happened, to the extent that some officers have seen their partners killed and lying in a pool of blood, despite the reality that their partner was never even hit.

During a life-threatening encounter, the focus of attention is switched to visual processing to gather as much information about the situation as possible. This might account for reported incidents of some people being able to visually track a bullet in flight. Much like a high-speed camera can record a bullet as it travels, the human visual system is capable of recording that quality of information. The speed at which information is being processed during a highly stressful or life-threatening encounter may actually change so as to potentially allow someone to "see" that amount of detail.

Dominant Response Takes Over

There have been many accounts of officers who have been involved in gun battles where there is no conscious recollection of the mechanics of drawing or firing a weapon. In their book *Deadly Force Encounters,* Artwohl and Christensen (1997) have studied many of the effects that officers have experienced during gunfights.

According to the authors, 74% of the officers reported that they responded "automatically" to a perceived threat, giving little or no conscious thought to their actions. Based on their research, they advocate for police officers to receive training in high-stress situations, while regularly practicing ways to develop coping mechanisms to compensate for perceptual memory distortions.

Their research findings align with the experiential thinking mode described by Epstein (1994) as the automatic, intuitive mode of information processing that operates by different rules from that of the rational mode that occurs automatically and effortlessly outside the awareness because that is its natural mode of operation, a mode that is far more efficient than conscious, deliberative thinking.

This has profound implications for training because experiential thinking is based on past experiences. Therefore, under sudden life-threatening stress, individuals will likely exhibit behavior based on past experiences that they will automatically produce without conscious thought. This means that there is a necessity to not only train officers in appropriate tactics but also to provide sufficient repetition under stress so that new behaviors will automatically take precedent over any previously learned, potentially inappropriate behaviors that they possessed before becoming an officer.

Another implication that leads to support of the concept of Reality-Based Training is that all tactically minded officers and trainers know, which represents the foundation for reliable performance in high-stress situations, is that information received from textbooks and lectures is of a different quality from information acquired from experience. Experientially derived knowledge is often more compelling and more likely to influence behavior than abstract knowledge.

This is especially critical in sudden, high-stress situations requiring instant physical performance. Abstract knowledge obtained in lectures and books can be very useful in rational-thinking mode situations such as formulating policies and analyzing.

In 1980, the American Psychiatric Association formally recognized the existence of a disorder, like what was often referred by the Military as a "battle fatigue," which became known as post-traumatic stress disorder (PTSD). Symptoms of the disorder include intrusive recollections, excessive stress arousal, withdrawal, numbing, and depression. Pierson (1989) claims that critical stress affects up to 87% of all emergency service workers at least once in their careers. Critical incident stress manifests itself physically, cognitively, and emotionally. Police officers are certainly included in this "emergency service workers" category.

Reality-Based Training instruction that subjects the participants to high levels of stress during training will help officers develop these coping mechanisms to compensate for perceptual and memory distortions. Officers should receive training in and regularly practice ways to control arousal levels during high-stress situations. One process, the combat breathing technique, has proven highly effective in this area.

Neurological Effects of Stress

Kosslyn and Koenig (1995) posit that a reaction to an aversion (fear) stimulus will have two major effects on cognitive processing. The first is that it will cause heightened attention to the triggering stimulus at the cost of attention to other stimuli and internal events. Second, there is something called the "jangle effect" in which the respondent will have difficulty with some forms of reasoning or problem-solving, especially verbal problem-solving. It follows that internal dialogue, which is essential to many people during problem-solving, is particularly vulnerable to "jangle."

Kosslyn and Koenig discovered that spatial problem-solving was unaffected by the "jangle effect" since it is processed in the right frontal cortex instead of the left. The right frontal cortex is responsible for visual imagery and visual problem-solving. The importance of the phenomenon of spatial problem-solving with its relation to experience-based training cannot be overstated.

It is largely unknown to what extent each individual officer may become affected by stress, but what is known is that without the correct combat conditioning, that is, a conditioning of fighting skills to the Unconscious Competence level, if he/she begins to feel afraid that he/she might be injured or die and the sympathetic nervous system becomes activated, he/she will not be operating at an optimal level.

Only a well-trained individual who has adopted the warrior mindset is likely to be able to control and minimize sympathetic nervous system arousal or function well under its influence. For someone who has not studied the realities of dangerous conflict or the effects of sympathetic nervous system arousal, he/she will misinterpret cues from his/her own physiology and fail to understand what is going on under such circumstances. Consequently, he/she will begin channeling mental energies into a downward spiral of self-deprecating beliefs and negative self-talk. It is predictable and understandable that access to skills, which have been merely integrated at the Conscious Competence level, will be seriously reduced or even eliminated altogether during an encounter where survival stress comes into play.

Fighting

When someone has chosen to fight, it is impossible to know if he/she wants to fight you to physically harm you, fight you with the intention of escaping, or fight you with the intention of taking your life. Although it is always a possibility that an opponent has lethal intentions, he/she was not born with this predisposition toward killing other human beings.

Lorenz (2002), a scientist specializing in animal behaviors, noticed that animals in nature fight differently against other species of animals than they do against their own kind. Rattlesnakes, for instance, will turn their fangs against non-rattlesnakes, but not against each other. They instead will wrestle. Similarly, piranha will fight against each other with raps of their tails. In fact, all animals in nature seem to possess an inhibition to killing their own.

An important distinction that must be drawn is where animals have been known to fight to the death while protecting territory or their young, even against their own kind. The distinction lies in the amount of force used in defense of territory or offspring. Death is often an unfortunate byproduct of the refusal of an intra-species opponent to submit or flee in the face of the defensive aggression. If the animals continue to fight, one may eventually die. The opponents use fighting methods that are not intended to be lethal, but instead to merely drive away the opponent. The relentless application of force, however, may finally result in death. An example of this occurs with headstrikes used by crocodiles defending their territory. Rather than turning their powerful jaws on one another, the intent of the headstrike is not to kill, but instead to drive the other away. Unfortunately, if you get hit sufficiently hard in the head enough times, it can kill you.

There will be those who argue with Lorenz's findings, pointing to pit bulls, or roosters used in cockfighting where killing is simply for sport. Surprisingly to many, these animals must be specially raised and trained to overcome their genetic resistance to killing their own. Aggressive pit bulls are bred with other aggressive pit bulls and then trained to fight to the death. The same is true of roosters. Humans, too, can be trained to overcome their resistance to killing their own, although it has been one of the great challenges of military leaders for eons. Lorenz points out that in any social species there are approximately 2% that are "predisposed toward psychopathic aggressive tendencies." This is not to say that the 2% who possess an aggressive nature are necessarily murderous psychopaths who will kill their own without remorse, but it does validate that there is a subset in our human fraternity that does not have the same level of genetic baggage when it comes to killing someone.

One thing of particular significance for law enforcement, as extrapolated from the military experience is this: if it is true that during open and declared warfare there are such high ratios of non-firers where the objective is clearly stated—find the enemy and kill them—then how much more difficult will it be for law enforcement officers to kill someone where the objective is not so clearly stated. A lethal engagement often begins as a surprise incident for law enforcement, and there may not be a clearly defined enemy before the beginning of an encounter. If it is indeed true that humans have a built-in resistance to killing another human being, it follows that killing, especially for law enforcement personnel, will likely be used as a last resort. What then is the first resort?

Posturing

Konrad Lorenz (2002) teaches us that the first choice during intra-species conflict comes down to the decision between fleeing and posturing. Only when the posturer has failed to dissuade his/her opponent do the options become fight, flee, or submit.

When confronted with interpersonal combat, although some people flee, posturing is usually the first choice, with the intent that posturing might lead to victory without fighting. It is always important to remind the officers in training that the Continuum of Force concept starts with "mere presence," which is the lowest level of use of force but can be effective in certain situations, if officers are trained in an appropriate manner. This lowest level of use of force is predicated upon the notion that officers represent the state authority. Officers need to develop personal skills in the use of coercion to control some kinds of problems (Skolnick and Fyfe 1993). The way we present ourselves to others can, in certain situations, make an enormous difference for the outcome of the situation.

References

Artwohl, D. A., & Christensen, L. W. (1997). *Deadly force encounters – What cops need to know to mentally and physically prepare for and survive a gunfight*. Boulder: Paladin Press.

Epstein, S. (1994). Integration of the cognitive and the psychodynamic unconscious. *American Psychologist, 49*(8), 709.

Haberfeld, M. R. (2018). *Critical issues in police training* (3rd ed.). Upper Saddle River: Pearson Custom Publishing.

Klinger, D. (2004). *Into the kill zone: A Cop's eye view of deadly force*. San Francisco: Jossey-Bass.

Kosslyn, S. M., & Koenig, O. (1995). *Wet mind: The new cognitive neuroscience*. New York: Free Press.

Kureczka, A. W. (1996). Critical incident stress in law enforcement. *FBI Law Enforcement Bulletin, 65*(3), 10–16.

Lorenz, K. (2002). *On aggression*. New York: Psychology Press.

Pierson, T. (1989, February). Critical incident stress: A serious law enforcement problem. (pp. 32–33). *The Police Chief*.

Siddle, B. K. (1995). *Sharpening the Warrior's edge*. Millstadt: PPCT Research Publications. www.ppct.com.

Skolnick, J. H., & Fyfe, J. J. (1993). *Above the law: Police and the excessive use of force* (pp. 198–205). New York: Free Press.

Vonk, K. (2004). *Heart rate as it relates to police performance under stress*. Michigan: Ann Arbor PD.

Chapter 4
Rules of Engagement: Addressing the "Unconsciously Incompetent" Mode Through Scenario-Based Training

When it comes to decidedly killing people, humans still want to follow rules and guidelines. For law enforcement officers, killing another human being is, and should be, serious business, and in a civilized society, there are good reasons for rules and regulations governing the use of lethal force. It is for this reason that our legal watchdogs constantly review the status of laws dealing with using force against others in light of the changing times. The Catch-22 for law enforcement is that while such laws impact heavily on law enforcers, those acting outside the law are not hampered by rules of engagement. Criminals have no use-of-force policies governing their actions, nor are they necessarily concerned about the terminal resting place of the bullets they fire. This gives the suspect an immense advantage in any type of encounter, leaving peacekeepers to play a deadly game of catch-up once the offender has decided the time for posturing is over.

Despite the desire to "rise above" the criminal element and temper the amount of force used, an officer must never lose sight of the fact that it is indeed possible that an opponent really does want to kill him/her, and when the moment of realization comes that he/she is suddenly in a fight for his/her life, it will be necessary to transcend the baggage of his/her own socialization if he/she is to level the playing field. In such cases, an officer must be "enabled" in advance to take a human life.

This enabling process includes overcoming the psychological safeguards that nature has imposed upon him/her. These limitations, or Killing Enabling Factors, include:

- Predisposition of the killer
- Demands of authority
- Distances between the killler and the victim
- Target attractiveness
- Group absolution

All these factors are dealt with in great detail in *On Killing*, and while they all play a part in limiting or enabling a killing behavior, for this book, I am going to

K. R. Murray, M. R. Haberfeld, *Use of Force Training in Law Enforcement*, SpringerBriefs in Criminology, https://doi.org/10.1007/978-3-030-59880-8_4

focus on two of the more important factors—predisposition of the killer, and the distances between the killer and the victim (Grossman 1995; Grossman and DeGaetano 1999).

This segment analyzes and contrasts Grossman's (1995), Grossman and DeGaetano (1999), and Grossman and Christensen (2004) *Killing Enabling Factors* from the perspective of Good Guys versus Bad Guys. Although both groups need to reconcile the Killing Enabling Factors before taking a life, an analysis of the socialization factors on the part of the Good Guys and the anti-socialization factors on the part of the Bad Guys will clearly show that the Bad Guys have a decided advantage.

The Dichotomy of Previous Killing Experience

There is no question that part of the job description of the military and law enforcement is to kill people under certain conditions. Still, some agencies instill in their officers a sense of dread over the prospect of taking a life. While the use of lethal force should be serious business, officers must have a clear sense of support from their agency if the use of lethal force becomes necessary. This, unfortunately, is often not the case as shown in the following theoretical example.

Let us assume for a moment that an officer revives his/her first gunfight, and that in a perfect world he/she remains in law enforcement after the shooting incident. After an amount of time the clouds have cleared, the legal battles have been fought and won, the psychological evaluations or any necessary PTSD treatment have been completed, and the officer is back on the street again.

Up pops another Bad Guy who, through his actions require the use of deadly force, is shot. Once again the officer is capable and is involved in the fight. Fortunately, the officer comes out of the situation unscathed. But what happens inside some agencies? There are some that may start thinking that there is a probem that needs to be addressed. However, let us assume the officer legally survives this second shooting and his/her career is unaffected. The officer eventually returns to full active duty.

Would not you know it … that very day, up comes Bad Guy number three, waving a gun at the officer. Our hero once again rises to the challenge, despite the fact that this officer has just shot three people, all justifiably, what is the likelihood he/she is going to be permitted by his/her agency to return to the street? According to Artwohl and Christensen (1997), this will vary from agency to agency.

Sensitivity Retraining

Because of high-profile incidents that have caused the media to focus their beam of societal concern on instances of police brutality and alleged abuses of power, many agencies implement programs designed to improve social interaction between officers and the public. However, cops are human, and being nice to someone who is not being nice back is unnatural. De-escalation training can only do that much. A recent encounter between a law enforcement officer and an unruly woman at a Florida airport, where the woman basically violates the personal space of the officer, while yelling and threatening, exemplifies the limits of training (Ovalle and Rabin 2020). Unfortunately, even the best training cannot always supersede human nature and the desire to push back when cornered. Yet, Reality-Based Training can help.

Rules of Engagement/Force Policy

All agencies have policies governing various uses of force. Officers are duty-bound to act within those policies, to the extent that officers acting within the law of the land may still be penalized for acting outside agency policy. Despite the fact that there has never been a single method of force outlawed by a court in America, officers in certain jurisdictions do not have the ability, through restrictive departmental policies, to use various force options. Pepper spray, certain types of impact weapons, electronic weapons, and various types of incapacitating physical interventions such as neck restraints have been prohibited by some agencies despite their popular use and effectiveness elsewhere.

Beyond the restrictions on tools and techniques, because of the way many officers interpret their force policies, many will often wait for an offender to "do something" before they "do something back." These officers do not understand that when employed properly, a force model can be used proactively rather than reactively. Unfortunately, a proactive use of force can be viewed as overly aggressive. Alternatively, using force reactively can lead to officer's injury and death, since action by an offender is always faster than reaction by an officer.

Because of lack of clarity from some agencies as to what is expected from an officer, many end up confused and frustrated with force policies. Much of the confusion is a direct result of how a force model is taught. Many of the force models look like a pyramid, a number line, a set of stairs, or a ladder. This creates the mistaken impression that there must be some sort of linear progression to the use of force. This is not the case. In fact, officers can skip any stage, based on the individual perception of danger (Skolnick and Fyfe 1993).

Because of this entrenched linear paradigm, force models are often taught in an extremely fragmented fashion leaving an incorrect residual belief that a force continuum is a "series" of possible events. Unfortunately, students do not get the message that a force continuum is not necessarily a force progression nor should it be considered so, since the situational requirements are rarely linear but dynamic in nature.

Artwohl and Christensen (1997) explain this concept using *The Rules of Holes*. That hole might not only be related to physical danger, but also to legal peril. Disengagement is important since officers must be able to articulate why they did not disengage after each and every use of force incident. Although it is rarely a necessity to actually disengage, it must be a consideration. Jeopardy to self or to others is always a reason to not disengage, but that reason must be articulated or at least articulable.

During any use-of-force, an officer has four choices and any of those options should be available at any time throughout the encounter:

- Continued application of the existing option
- Escalation
- De-escalation
- Disengagement

Whichever force model is taught, the major downfall is often the method in which it is taught. Consequently, students often fail to realize who exactly is making the decision as to which level of force is to be applied, and often have difficulty grasping the concept that it is not the officer who is choosing the force level but the offender.

Officers often wind up confused and caught behind the power curve because their training has not provided them with an experiential model for interpreting behavioral threat cues. Because of this experiential deficiency, officers are often unclear as to when the "fight is on," and while it is not usually up to the officer whether or not the fight is on, it is essential for him/her to recognize when it is.

This is part of the real value of Reality-Based Training. If properly structured, Reality-Based Training can be utilized to teach experience-based decision-making that is in line with the departmental use-of-force model. *Training at the Speed of Life*™ – *Volume III (Murray* 2015) provides a series of drills and exercises for teaching a force continuum in an experiential way. These drills ensure that officer actions are calibrated with real events rather than some intellectual model that exists in a book or on a television screen. This will also help ensure that there is no misunderstanding of what the Bad Guy is asking for, and that there is no misunderstanding of departmental policy about what "level of customer service" should be given to the Bad Guy in return.

Given the reality that the vast majority of modern day law enforcement officers are not schooled in the fighting arts, it is safe to assume that they are also not schooled in the dynamics of conflict, so they will have trouble "reading" an opponent. Misreading a suspect's intentions and overlooking his/her "pre-attack" cues can be devastating.

RBT helps students to decode human behavior so that proper responses can be applied to aggressive behaviors. One excellent training system to help achieve that goal is Tony Blauer's (2020) TCMS (Tactical Confrontation Management System). Blauer's comprehensive program consists of:

Emotional Climate Drill™

- Explores the emotion connection to fear, flinching, and tactics
- Helps officers to recognize why, where, and when they might hesitate
- Develops pain management and resolute focus

Emotional Motion Drill™

- Empirical process to show how "emotions" can influence tactics
- Allows officers to "defuse" themselves during training and incidents

Live Action Response Drill™

- Empirically teaches appropriateness
- Cultivates the use of the Three Is: Intuition, Instinct, and Intelligence
- Re-affirms the officer's role and rules of engagement

Ballistic Micro-Fight™

- Final phase in development
- Improves "task" specific [muscular, mental] endurance and stamina
- Creates the real life blueprint through the replication process (victim to victor transition)

Utilizing a comprehensive and progressive training system such as Blauer's TCMS will help students understand when a fight is on and when to switch gears from posturing to fighting, since to be successful it is essential to have a thorough understanding of the mechanics of conflict. Here, Grossman (1995), Grossman and DeGaetano (1999) is extremely helpful as it dissects the four options during a confrontation – Fight, Flee, Posture, or Submit.

The important thing to understand is that a suspect who is not completely under control can change behavioral channels at any moment. Before gaining submission, however, there are some behavioral cues that suggest which modality he/she is in. If he/she has not submitted and is not fleeing, then he/she is either posturing (attempting to defeat you through non-aggressive means) or fighting. Either is unacceptable, and an officer should, at this stage, be using some measure of force suitable for countering the level of resistance.

Boyd's Loop, part of the OODA concept (Observe, Orient, Decide, Act, 2020) meshes perfectly with the "Fight, Flight, Submit, and Posture" model. By taking action, it forces the suspect back into observation mode. If continuous actions are taken to dominate and overwhelm a suspect, he/she is never afforded the opportunity to make it through his/her decision-making loop because he/she is never permitted an opportunity to effectively get through the orientation phase of the decision-making process. He/she remains "disoriented." As stated earlier – no orientation, no decision. No decision, no action. Consequently, continuous action on the part of the officer ends up being safer for all concerned parties. The appropriate level of action or force is the only questionable factor here, and it can only be addressed through training and a thorough understanding of departmental policy.

When it comes to a potentially lethal engagement where a suspect is holding a weapon, the possible force options become limited, so the employment of those options must be swift and decisive. Officers require a high level of experience during such an encounter to ensure a successful resolution. Of all the situations, as observed by one of the authors during Reality-Based Training, those involving a suspect holding a weapon have produced the most interesting material and the liveliest of discussions. The point of contention seems to be between the perception of a threat and the immediacy of a threat.

While posturing can sometimes lead to a successful resolution without the need for force, it is extremely dangerous (yet exceedingly common) for officers to get "stuck" in posturing mode. Officers are not being paid to lose, so posturing moments should be brief and should primarily consist of directing a suspect's actions and stating the consequences for not following those directions. There may be times when an officer will have the luxury of protracted negotiations with a suspect, but this can only occur where the officer has control of all the external circumstances of the incident. Even if he/she has time, distance, cover, and confidence in his/her abilities, the focus of any verbal communication should be the clear statement of the only possible choices that the suspect has, such as "Drop the weapon or I will shoot you," or "Do not turn around holding that weapon or I will shoot you."

If, after hearing the command and the consequences of inaction, the suspect still refuses to drop the weapon, the officer should consider the following:

1. The suspect's posturing has not and will not succeed.
2. The suspect is not fleeing.
3. The suspect has not submitted to direct commands and is unfazed by consequences that the officer has explained.

Even factoring in the other two possibilities for a suspect who is not actively engaged in fight, hiding or stalling, it must be assumed that hiding has failed because there is actually an encounter underway, and stalling will not succeed since there is no possible successful solution that can result from it. It is also possible that a suspect is stalling because his/her decision-making process is being overwhelmed and he/she has not yet realized the futility of his/her actions, or he/she is absolutely clueless as to the fact that he/she is doing anything wrong and is about to be shot. Either way, since posturing will not succeed, stalling must eventually give way to fighting or submitting.

Officers must prepare for the likelihood that once a suspect's posturing fails and he/she has not run away or is not submitting, then he/she is looking for an opportunity to fight, and if he/she has a pistol in his/her hand, that means he/she is probably going to try to shoot at you. It is just that simple … be ready.

One of the decisive factors on whether the suspect will have to be shot will be the availability and use of cover, availability of extended range impact weapons, whether the suspect thinks he/she has a chance of winning, his/her willingness to die, or other such mitigating considerations. Unfortunately, cover is often only a consideration after the bullets have started to fly, if at all. Training that helps to make the use of cover a conditioned response will go a long way to reducing the necessity to shoot a suspect as well as helping officers prevail during a critical encounter. Extended range impact weapons will usually only arrive during a protracted incident, so they may not always be a viable option. A suspect's perception of being able to win will also be directly based on the number and demeanor of officers present.

Another decisive factor on whether an officer will shoot in such a situation is the support that an officer believes he/she will get from his/her agency in the event of a shooting. For a more detailed explanation dealing with the effects of support from those in authority, Grossman's books *On Killing* and *On Combat* go into greater detail in dealing with the Killing Enabling Factors. In *On Killing*, he has an entire section dedicated to the Proximity and Demands of Authority. Having support from the department can be critical to how an officer performs under demanding circumstances.

One final note before moving on is that sometimes, because of a lack of confidence or physical ability, an officer will take extraordinary measures to avoid the fight altogether and become the Reluctant Warrior. It is essential to have "Fit for Duty" policies that provide for removing an officer from the street if they are incapable of engaging violent suspects, especially if they are unwilling or unable to use lethal force if necessary to deal with those situations.

Teaching a force model using Low-Level Scenarios and testing an officer's abilities to apply appropriate levels of force in accordance with law and policy through the use of High-Level Scenarios will assist training staff in learning whether they have a Reluctant Warrior in their midst. There are a large number of officers who have internalized the belief that they must do "whatever it takes to go home at the end of a shift." While this sounds like a sound officer safety philosophy, sadly it is often a cop-out many would use to justify not putting themselves in harm's way in the defense of someone they have sworn an oath to protect.

Many such officers believe that the hierarchy of those who must be protected is:

- Themselves
- The person being victimized
- Anyone else in harm's way
- The perpetrator

Many officers have been injured or killed as a result of such a mindset, and sensible administrators must ensure there are rules of engagement written into their force policies to protect officers from being unnecessarily placed in harm's way, especially for the benefit of a known criminal.

Justification to Use Lethal Force Versus the Necessity to Use Lethal Force

There will be times when there will be justification for certain advanced levels of force, yet officers choose lower levels. This is often the case during lethal force encounters where officers are justified in shooting someone, but they choose not to. Just because an officer does not shoot a suspect when he/she is justified does not necessarily make him/her the Reluctant Warrior.

During scenario training, tenuous situations like this often occur and highlight the necessity for trainers to make sure whatever action a student either takes or does not take is justifiable based on the information the student is processing. It is not unusual to have two officers come to opposite conclusions and have both be completely justified. Trainers must be prepared for this reality and make sure that they do not pre-judge a student based simply upon his/her actions.

High-quality simulation training will help you determine whether an officer has the capacity to use lethal force and will also provide insight on the makeup of an individual officer's personal force continuum. As an instructor, you have a duty to learn the skills necessary to properly observe and debrief students to determine why an officer took the actions he/she did. Despite your belief that he/she should or should not have shot a suspect (or employed other force measures) based on how the scenario was written or on your own training and experience, actions taken by the student might be completely reasonable predicated upon what he/she was experiencing. Often, an Exercise Controller will fail a student for not shooting during a scenario where there was "justification" for that shooting, or if it was specifically written as a "shoot" scenario. There are times when justification to use lethal force is at direct odds with necessity to use lethal force encounter.

Another complication stems from the all too frequent occurrences where suspects are choosing "suicide by cop." These days, it is not only important, but now a legal requirement that agencies provide training for dealing with an emotionally disturbed individual who might be seeking to have the police end his/her life for him/her.

Hand in hand with the legal determination that agencies must be prepared to deal with self-destructive offenders is the growing problem of actions taken by an officer that unnecessarily escalates the danger to the point where lethal force seems necessary. All too often, officers end up creating their own jeopardy, and later make an attempt to justify a lethal force encounter by testifying they had "no choice" because the suspect was exhibiting dangerous behaviors consistent with the application of lethal force.

In the case of Allen v. Muskogee (1997), Mr. Allen was despondent and suicidal. Officers at the scene rushed to the vehicle he was sitting in and attempted to take a pistol away from him. Shots were exchanged and Mr. Allen was killed. The shooting was deemed justifiable at trial, but the 10th Circuit court of appeals overturned that finding. The city of Muskogee was found in violation of the 4th Amendment, and the shooting of Mr. Allen was deemed unjustified. One of the issues was that responding officers have a duty to not create their own jeopardy through leaving cover and approaching such individuals where jeopardy does not already immediately exist. The court further found that agencies must have training in dealing with emotionally disturbed or suicidal persons, and those that do not are "out of step with the rest of the nation."

In the Allen case, there was no testimony that any such pattern existed, nor was there any evidence indicating that the training of the agency for such situations was inadequate.

This case is noteworthy for two important reasons. First, the Allen case sets a precedent that it is essential for agencies to have some sort of Crisis Intervention Training (CIT) such as the Memphis Model in an effort to avoid killing emotionally disturbed individuals (Watson and Fulambarker 2012).

Second, in many training simulations where officers have created their own jeopardy similar to the Allen situation, they have subsequently shot the suspect, only to be lauded by the training staff. In the section of this book dealing with how to set up and run training simulations, the point is, that in the Allen case, the dissenting justice disagreed based on the lack of a pattern of civil rights violations. It might sound like a long-shot, but if agencies can successfully argue that RBT provides valuable lethal force experience due to the level of reality inherent in the training, then it may be possible to argue that the repetition of a training scenario that demonstrates a violation of law or policy could constitute a "pattern of constitutional violations" and that "continued adherence to its training thus constitutes deliberate indifference."

Whether an officer finds him/her self living out a litigation nightmare such as Allen v. Muskogee, experience and situational awareness will play key factors in such situations, and the experience gained from training for such situations is probably the best argument that can be used to obtain more training time and money, as well as underscores the need to tighten up training so that it is in line with departmental policy and public safety requirements.

Spontaneous, Deliberate Lethal Force, and Reactive Lethal Force

Anecdotal and empirical data demonstrates that training and experience make the difference between spontaneous lethal force, deliberate lethal force, and reactive lethal force. Spontaneous lethal force occurs where force is employed as an immediate and unconscious response to the perception of a lethal force stimulus where officers often have no conscious recollection of the decision to draw and fire. Deliberate lethal force occurs where, in the presence of justification, additional factors become conscious considerations. Reactive lethal force occurs where force is employed as an immediate reflexive response where justification may not be present and is not a conscious consideration. Reactive lethal force can be likened to a flinch response in response to a frightening event.

Ideally, an officer should be capable of both spontaneous and deliberate, but should train to avoid reactive. Spontaneous lethal force is distinguished from reactive lethal force, and it is possible only where skills have been sufficiently conditioned to the Unconscious Competence level permitting immediate response to an instantaneous lethal threat. Deliberate lethal force is possible where there are a sufficient number of mitigating circumstances to create a time and distance buffer. When there is time, distance, and cover available to provide that overall buffer, the hairline difference between an immediate threat and an imminent threat can prove to be the decisive factors between a shooting that is deemed justified and one that is not. Unfortunately, reactive lethal force is often employed and has led to innocents being killed or seriously wounded.

A recent change in the California Use of Force Policy (2019) exemplifies the problematic nature of "immediate threat" versus "imminent threat." The new policy, AB392, the bill signed into law by Gov. Gavin Newsom and became effective on January 1, 2020, modified the conditions under which a police officer can legally use deadly force from times when it is "reasonable" to when it is "necessary."

Legal experts say the spirit of the measure—encouraging de-escalation and crisis-intervention methods—clearly attempts to induce greater restraint from officers. However, it would also require an immediate retraining of the officers in the concepts of "reasonable" versus "necessary" (Ortiz 2019).

Immediate Versus Imminent

In an opinion paper written by Tom Aveni of the Police Policy Studies Center entitled *The Must-Shoot/May Shoot Controversy*, he discusses the difference between immediate and imminent in light of a police shooting:

> Quite often, the underlying cause of misunderstanding in 'May-Shoot' scenarios is embedded within our mistaken assumption that "imminent" threats are synonymous with "immediate" threats. From a legal and policy perspective, you can drive a truck through the difference. As referenced previously, an immediate threat is one that is ongoing. Literally, the possibility of mortal injury is immediate. By accepted legal definition, the word 'imminent' is characterized as follows: Threatened actions or outcomes that *may* occur during an encounter. Threatened harm does not have to be instantaneous. An *immediate* threat is measured in finite terms of time. It is NOW. As imminence is defined above, it is NOT defined in terms that are clearly finite. Indeed, imminence is 'elastic' in time. How important is that distinction? As was stated from the outset, we routinely see in-policy and out-of-policy shootings separated by micro measurements of time. An imminent threat is often one that is *perceived* to be unfolding. Quite often, that perception is mired in ambiguity. Many 'May-Shoot' scenarios occur under low light conditions where sensory stimuli are often muddled so severely that they heighten situational uncertainty. Almost as many occur in high-risk situations in which suspects disregard verbal commands and engage in furtive movements.

The courts have held officers to the standard of imminent danger instead of immediate danger when they choose to employ lethal force. This notwithstanding, since the difference between an in-policy and an out-of-policy shooting can often be measured in fractions of a second and will be based on the totality of the circumstances perceived by the officer on the scene. Clearly, an officer's situational awareness can make the difference between firing and not firing. Situational awareness, as we learned earlier, can be directly attributed to experience, and before an officer's first real lethal force encounter, experience in this area can only be attributed to Reality-Based Training.

David Klinger (2004) interviewed officers who have prevailed during lethal encounters. One of the interesting aspects of his book is the number of officers who have held their fire under circumstances where shootings were clearly justified. Klinger's book details the accounts of officers who processed immense amounts of detail, and he describes the decision processes—the crystal clear thinking—that can occur within the precious few seconds that are characteristic of many lethal force encounters. In many of the instances he wrote about, there was clearly the capacity for cognitive thought despite the chaotic and often frightening circumstances. It seems that during many of the occurrences, the timeframe, while certainly important, will run a distant second to the training and experience of the shooter. The amount of sensory input that can be processed within such a compressed timeframe is staggering, but such an ability to process that information is always dependent upon an officer's situational awareness – predicated upon experience and training.

Jeopardy is an extremely subjective area, and it is not only possible but highly likely that two officers in the exact same situation will see and process different information. This is the very reason that most tactical teams participate in after action reviews following tactical operations, and why critical incident debriefs are essential following any critical incident.

Often, those who are uncomfortable with this "holding back" will argue that when a suspect creates justification for lethal force, he/she should be shot and those who do not pull the trigger in such instances create greater jeopardy for themselves and for others. They further argue that when lethal force is justified, those who hold back are suffering from some defect of character or training. This is indeed possible, but the opposite should not be ignored ... that those who hold back at the point of legal justification may indeed be possessed of a high degree of training, and possessed of sound character. They may not be the Reluctant Warrior, but instead may be the Enlightened Warrior. It comes down to the question of what exactly constitutes personal jeopardy or jeopardy to others, and what specific information the officer was processing during his decision-making. Surely there are clear-cut cases where it is necessary to employ lethal force, and in such cases that force should be employed with great speed and efficiency. But there are also instances where, in the face of clear justification, restraint is possible based upon mitigating factors. The important thing from a training perspective is that the staff must be trained to properly debrief a student on exactly why he/she did what he/she did or did not do because it is vital to ascertain which type of warrior you have in your midst ... Reluctant or Enlightened. It is in the dubious situations where training and experience may make the difference, and the Balance of Restraint may be the deciding factor between necessity versus mere justification, or perhaps even between application of justice versus dispensation of vengeance.

Unclear Force Policies

Reality-Based Training will help highlight policy deficiencies that exist in some agencies, since during RBT an officer may exhibit tactically questionable behaviors. During the debrief, it is often possible to discover that an agency has holes in its use of force or officer safety policies.

An example occurred during a training scenario in which a lone officer got into a firefight with a suspect. Immediately following the shooting, the officer holstered his weapon and approached the down suspect. During the debrief, the officer was asked to justify his immediate movement from a covered position to single-handedly dealing with someone he had just "shot." His response was that according to departmental policy, he had a responsibility to immediately treat an injured party although it may pose a danger to himself. Unless I am specifically hired to do so, it is not my position to second-guess departmental policies, but in this case the officer's actions raised questions about his agency's officer safety procedures. During an after action review, the issue was raised with other members of the same department, precipitating some lively discussion that highlighted some conflicting views on their policies and procedures with injured suspects. As it turned out, the agency had no clear policy on what should be done in such a situation, but it was obvious that rendering aid to someone who had just been shot, while desirable if there are others there to ensure the scene is safe, was foolhardy given the imminent danger to a single officer. Since that time, they have developed new policies consistent with officer safety principles and in line with public policy issues.

Since most policies have been developed in response to previous costly errors, it follows that there are agencies that will lack policy in certain areas where they have not experienced any suffering, either financial (lawsuits) or emotional (loss of officers or members of the public.) Proactive trainers must be on the lookout for dangerous trends that are occurring regionally and nationally so they can create new and useful policies, and then conduct training to ensure their department-wide implementation. Reality-Based Training is an excellent test bed for discovering policy deficiencies if the training staff is alert to their occurrences.

If this approach to policy development and method for teaching force options within a well established use-of-force policy sounds complicated and time consuming, you are partially right. Much will depend on the amount of administrative inconsistency or lack of procedural guidance that currently exists in your agency and how much departmental resistance there is going to be to achieve clarification. In many instances, it is going to take a lot of time and effort to sort out the inconsistencies but once they are sorted out and Reality-Based Training standards are implemented, there will be a much more cohesive approach being taken with regard to justifiable uses of force that are in line with predictable officer responses to specific suspect actions. The end result will be fewer liability concerns for the agency and a much safer working environment for the officers.

A force model, if improperly understood, will create a huge disadvantage for an officer and provide an immense tactical advantage to the offender. Just remember that historically, when one side has rules and the other side does not, things can be extremely hazardous for the "got rules" side especially if the "got rules" side is unclear about exactly what is expected of them.

Reactive

Because of misunderstood force policies, officers tend to be reactive rather than proactive and quite slow in those reactions. Most of this can be directly attributed to an absence of programmed responses to specific threats.

Officers can get stuck in the observation phase of Boyd's Loop because they often literally "cannot believe their eyes." They see something happening, but lapse into what Gavin de Becker (2002) calls denial, and what John Farnam calls the verification mindset (Farnam 1994). While stuck in denial, it is impossible to begin effectively orienting as to which of the various response options are viable for the current situation. This is the primary purpose of connecting possible offender stimuli to certain force options by using Low-Level Scenarios to program a dominant response. Having a dominant response programmed will also help combat the denial mindset.

If an officer has programmed a dominant response for a specific threat stimulus, according to the principles taught by Col. Boyd and Mike Spick (1988), he/she should be able to respond quickly and decisively since Observation (threat recognition through previous experiential training) will be virtually immediate, Orientation/Decision will be a programmed event based on stimulus/response style training, and the Action will be smooth and efficient if it has been practiced to the extent that a torque profile has been created.

Situational awareness, as described by Mike Spick in *The Ace Factor* (1988), accounted for wide margins of success following a relatively small number of decisive combat engagements. These decisive engagements do not have to be real-life engagements. The effect can be accomplished using advanced simulation techniques such as described above, through advanced simulator technologies or through a combination of technologies used in concert. Several years ago, SGI (Silicon Graphics) developed a simulator for pilot training that was so realistic that pilots emerged from the simulator sessions drenched in sweat.

Spick's findings are supported by those of Top Gun, the Navy's Fighter Weapons School. At Top Gun, participants go head to head against opposing forces in simulated combat missions using actual aircraft fitted with advanced technology to record the events. This realistic approach to training has been shown to develop a highly sophisticated situational awareness in fighter pilots. Similarly, participants in properly structured Reality-Based Training simulations have achieved high levels of situational awareness. Before "facing the flames" of actual combat, RBT is the only truly effective method for providing the necessary stress inoculations to dangerous situations. In the pursuit of such stress inoculation, however, strong caution must be urged. One of the functions of RBT is to attempt to reduce the reactive nature of shootings. Well-intentioned, yet ill-conceived methods of attempting to inoculate officers must be cautioned against. Tom Aveni (2003) of the Police Policy Studies Council, in his report *Officer-Involved Shootings: What We Didn't Know Has Hurt Us*, suggests that while research into so-called "stress inoculation" might hold promise for the enhancement of future police gunfight efficacy, this concept cannot be pursued haphazardly. The employment of so-called "shoot-houses" or "kill-houses" has been seen as a means to achieve handgun proficiency while inoculating officers to the stress of worldly dangers.

In reality, heavy reliance on such tools may give officers a distorted predisposition in using their handguns as a primary tool for problem-solving. Instead of the "house of horrors" approach to handgun training, agencies should be pursuing handgun training that represents an all-encompassing "conflict resolution" methodology. Scenario-based training is essential, and it should seldom culminate in gunfire.

Many experiences of "shoot-houses" are glorified experiences. They are not exercises in judgmental shooting. Instead, they are exercises in reactive shooting against pre-set lethal threat targets. Training staff expects the officer to "kill" all such threats that exist inside that environment. Although well-intentioned, this style of training may turn soldiers into "house cleaners" if not carefully designed, and does little to prepare police officers for the realities they are likely to encounter. It may not reliably improve their ability to make sound lethal force decisions under difficult circumstances. In fact, it may achieve just the opposite. It may begin to program a higher level of reactivity into an already reactive officer to fire as quickly as possible at whatever comes into his field of vision. We must be careful with how a shoot house experience is organized and why.

Hesitation

Much of the problem with the concept of hesitation stems from not having programmed a response to the situation which is unfolding, uncertainty as to the law, belief systems that have not yet been sorted out, fear of being sued or criminally prosecuted for actions taken, administrative actions against officers involved in previous shootings, and the genetic coding against lethal action that for most people is not yet understood. When faced with a lethal force decision, even in training where there are no real consequences in making a bad decision, many officers needlessly hesitate despite the presence of clear justification and necessity. This will often occur without any intellectual basis as to why, although many report that it is in no small way related to fear of departmental reprisal or other consequences of action. The preoccupation with personal consequences that might arise out of taking action against a suspect can have devastating effects on performance.

Hesitation is a real problem and will continue to be one until departments give officers a much clearer mandate on the use of force, and until officers come to terms with all of the factors that weigh in during a lethal force encounter. The only way to accomplish this is through education on the issues and through Reality-Based Training that places officers in the situations where the various force options must be applied. Only then will there be a truly effective teaching model for decisive action in the face of danger. Certainly, the most recent developments in the calls for changes in use-of-force policies by local departments (Muggah and Abt 2020) will contribute, in the most profound manner, to the ways police trainers deal with the hesitation concept.

We should however continue to rely on social and behavioral research or enhance our training options. In recent years, Andersen et al. (2018) studied the error rates of police officers in their application of deadly force. Their reseach explored the possibility of improving police health and safety outcomes by targeting physiological regulation during stress, and enhancing recovery following threatening encounters. The findings from this study seem very promising and emphasize, even further, the need to incorporate empirical research findings into the tactical training of use of force.

References

Allen v. Muskogee, 119 F.3d 837 (10th Cir. 1997).

Andersen, J. P., Di Nota, P. M., Beston, B., Boychuk, E. C., Gustafsberg, H., Poplawski, S., & Arpaia, J. (2018). Reducing lethal force errors by modulating police physiology. *Journal of Occupational and Environmental Medicine, 60*(10), 867.

Artwohl, D. A., & Christensen, L. W. (1997). *Deadly force encounters – What cops need to know to mentally and physically prepare for and survive a gunfight.* Boulder: Paladin Press.

Aveni, T. J. (2003). Officer-involved shootings: What we didn't know has hurt us. *The Police Policy Studies Council, 4*, 15–16.

Blauer, T. (2020). *Tactical Management System.* Retrieved from: https://blauerspear.com/about, July 24, 2020.

Boyd, J. (2020). *The OODA Loop and the half- beat.* Retrieved from: https://thestrategybridge.org/the-bridge/2020/3/17/the-ooda-loop-and-the-half-beat; July 24, 2020.

De Becker, G. (2002). *Fear less: Real truth about risk, safety, and security in a time of terrorism.* Boston: Little, Brown and Company.

Farnam, J. S. (1994). *The Farnam method of defensive Handgunning.* Onalaska: Firearms Academy of Seattle.

Grossman, D. (1995). *On killing: The psychological cost of learning to kill in war and society.* Boston: Little Brown.

Grossman, D., & Christensen, L. W. (2004). *On combat: The psychology and physiology of deadly conflict in war and in peace.* Millstadt: PPCT Research Publications.

Grossman, D., & DeGaetano, G. (1999). *Stop teaching our kids to kill : A call to action against TV, Movie & Video Game Violence.* New York: Crown Publishers.

Klinger, D. (2004). *Into the kill zone: A Cop's eye view of deadly force.* San Francisco: Jossey-Bass.

Muggah, R., & Abt, T. (2020). *Calls for Police reform are getting louder—Here is how to do it.* Retrieved July 24, 2020, https://foreignpolicy.com/2020/06/22/calls-for-police-reform-are-getting-louder-here-is-how-to-do-it/

Murray K. (2015). Unpublished training materials.

Ortiz, J. (2019). California's new police use-of-force law marks a 'significant' change in law enforcement. *Here's why.* Retrieved, July 24, 2020, https://www.usatoday.com/story/news/nation/2019/08/20/california-new-police-use-force-law-significant-change/2068263001/

Ovalle, D., & Rabin, C. (2020). Miami-Dade cop relieved of duty for hitting woman taunting him for "acting like you wite." *Miami Herald,* July 2, 2020.

Skolnick, J. H., & Fyfe, J. J. (1993). *Above the law: Police and the excessive use of force* (pp. 198–205). New York: Free Press.

Spick, M. (1988). *The ace factor : Air combat and the role of situational awareness.* Annapolis: Naval Institute Press.

Watson, A. C., & Fulambarker, A. J. (2012). The crisis intervention team model of police response to mental health crises: A primer for mental health practitioners. *Best Practices in Mental Health, 8*(2), 71.

Chapter 5
The Killing Experience: Unlikely Suspension of Judgment and Time Out for Safety

Since the period following the end of the Vietnam War, which saw a flood of people coming into law enforcement with some experience in the taking of human life, there are not a great deal of officers entering the field of law enforcement with up-close killing experience. While the skirmishes that America has been involved in since 9/11 have provided some limited experience in the area of killing, pound for pound the number of conditioned killers entering the law enforcement arena are proportionally insignificant. In fact, just the opposite is happening in many cases. Many specialized soldiers rotating out of military life have a difficult time finding work in the field of law enforcement. "Too aggressive…" many agencies believe. The psychological scales used during recruitment can identify some of the more aggressive tendencies in applicants, and even if these applicants are well-adjusted and have the ability to harness and focus their aggression for the betterment of society, they are summarily dismissed from many of the hiring processes. Further, many of the more aggressive and tactically minded individuals and existing police officers are actually leaving to take highly lucrative overseas contracts in the wake of the war on terror. Yet, other agencies are actively looking for the discharged military personnel, not necessarily for their use-of-force skills but based on the assumption that military training is similar to law enforcement and, therefore, these candidates are already vetted as suitable for the job (Barrett et al. 2009; Haberfeld et al. 2015; Haberfeld 2016, 2017).

Learning to become effective in the use of deadly force is a process that takes psychological conditioning and practice. By filtering out those who are more aggressive and those who have already received some conditioning in the act of killing, each new wave of officers hitting the streets is likely to have received no meaningful preparation for killing should they enter into the lethal force arena.

© The Author(s), under exclusive licence to Springer Nature Switzerland AG 2021   41
K. R. Murray, M. R. Haberfeld, *Use of Force Training in Law Enforcement*,
SpringerBriefs in Criminology, https://doi.org/10.1007/978-3-030-59880-8_5

Routine Experiences

According to the FBI KILOD reports (FBI, Press Release 2020), the routine, day-to-day, bread and butter of law enforcement situations that contribute to most of the line-of-duty deaths, include:

- Vehicle stops
- Investigative functions
- Tactical situations
- Unprovoked attacks
- Crimes in progress
- Assiting other law enforcement

Ambush situations seem to have been steadily on the increase. Unlike other situations where there is usually some pre-indicative behavior of high-end danger during the posturing phase of a face-to-face encounter, during an ambush, the killer has already decided to take a life. Most of an officer's survival at this point will be evenly split between the suspect's skill-at-arms, luck, and the officer's determination to win and survive (Walker et al. 2011).

A complacent mindset is difficult to overcome for those that consider themselves "friendly people." This is exactly what the hijackers on the ill-fated flights of September 11, 2001 counted on when they seized control of several aircraft using butter knives and box cutters. Despite the likelihood that the passengers could have overwhelmed the hijackers if they had decided to take action *en masse*, the hijackers were able to use simple weapons and intimidation to take and maintain control of the passengers and crew who were civilized people, and who were unprepared to rise up against the vastly inferior number of attackers who ultimately flew them to their doom. High-level predators will make a tactical use of any show of weakness, including fear or friendliness.

Officers must develop a "professional switch" to provide courteous service when necessary and an aggressive response when attacked. They must be ever vigilant, remembering that there is no such thing as a routine call. They must hone an "anticipation mindset" to counteract the complacency mindset. Once developed, the officer's subconscious perceptual radar will be forever scanning the environment for threat cues and will alert him/her to danger, often before it is consciously obvious to him/her. Some people call this "intuition." Crank (2014) refers to this intuitive approach as the "six sense suspicion." Intuition is not a psychic phenomenon. Instead, it is a tuning of the perceptual filters that we all have so that when a danger cue is picked up it is actually registered with the conscious mind, so we can quickly shift our attention to that stimulus. Tuning these filters requires experience and practice which can only be derived from actual encounters or high-quality Reality-Based Training (RBT).

Rarely Have to Go One-on-One for Very Long

With limited exceptions, most law enforcement skirmishes attract assistance pretty quickly. Most of the larger agencies even have buttons on top of their radios that an officer can press for help if he/she cannot communicate in other ways. Although it is reassuring to know that help is on the way, even two minutes is a long time when you are in a fight, whether you are winning or losing. Unless an officer has done some endurance training or knows how to conserve energy during a fight, he/she will be exhausted in less than two minutes. Fortunately, most agencies dispatch multiple officers to many of the statistically high-risk situations, lessening the likelihood of having to go one-on-one with an offender. The mere presence of a second officer is often enough to deter a suspect who might otherwise attack a lone officer.

Sterile Training

Given the high probability of an officer having to physically subdue suspects on a fairly regular basis, it would seem natural that those officers would have a substantial amount of training in the physical arts including full-contact practice fights (while using protective gear). It is surprising to most people that the majority of those who recently entered law enforcement have never been in an actual fistfight and, with the current trend against full-contact training in many agencies and academies, likely do not understand the physical implications of getting punched until some street cretin smacks them for the first time. Knowing what it feels like to get hit, and learning how not to get hit, are important life-skills for law enforcement. Yet, they are often avoided in the interest of safe training.

There must always be a balance between safety and realism in training, but things have gone too far on the side of safety as a result of some preventable injuries that have occurred in the past. Whenever an officer gets hurt in training, many agencies have a knee-jerk reaction and choose to eliminate the type of training that caused the injury, rather than modify the safety measures to eliminate that avoidable danger in the future.

Negative Training Experiences

Somewhere along the line, trainers think that providing a horrific experience in which an officer is ruled "dead" at the conclusion of a scenario will somehow help him/her perform better on the street. There is a fine line between challenging a student at a stressful level and overwhelming the student. Negative training experiences can program an officer for future failure and must be avoided.

Negative Media Exposure

Just as the Bad Guys can do everything wrong and get sympathetic media coverage, the Good Guys can do everything right and get poor media coverage. Living in the social media bite world that we do, 30 minutes of excellent tactical explanations of the mechanics and necessity of an operation can be pared down to a five-second quip taken out of context to further whatever real agenda the media had in the first place.

An example of questionable media practices occurred after a suspect took over a bus containing 13 disabled students and held the police at bay for hours while threatening to blow up the bus and the kids. Despite the fact that it was later learned that there was no bomb, the threat seemed credible and pulling off such a successful SWAT mission without injury to the kids was highly commendable. When the suspect was finally killed by SWAT, a cameraman got a shot of two SWAT officers high-fiving (Baltimore Sun 1995), framing the two officers with the corpse in the same picture. Saving those kids was a cause for a celebration, and that is exactly what those officers were doing. In more recent years, the number of negative images of police-citizens interactions, presented by the media around the United States and the world, are just too numeorus to account for and reference (Denef et al. 2013; Haberfeld 2019).

Training: Them

Experience Is the Best Teacher

It is inarguable that the run-of-the-mill street criminal has lots of life experience. In many cases, he has to fend for himself most of his life—if not physically, then at least emotionally, given the breakdown in the family unit. But it is not just the stereotypical Bad Guy that commits violent crimes. We now live in an era where "the quiet, shy" upper-middle class kid will steal daddy's gun or purchase it legally, or not, and go on a shooting rampage (Shultz et al. 2013; Levine and McKnight 2017).

Training: Us

With a cutback in funding across the board and an increased demand for a kinder, gentler officer, much of the high-liability training focuses on conflict avoidance or resolution through non-aggressive intervention (Scottie 2020).

The shape of things to come? We would like to hope not, yet the adage that "society gets the law enforcement it demands and the criminal it deserves" seems to be ringing true in this day and age. Some agencies have lost sight of the fact that the operative word in law enforcement is "enforcement," and the root word of enforcement is "force." Society seems to be demanding smaller, more docile police officers. Unfortunately, the criminal element seems unimpressed by the new genre of kinder and gentler officers. The costs in terms of officer injuries and officers killed in the line of duty are beginning to mount.

With cutbacks in high-liability training and multimillion-dollar projects being funded to find the next "Smart Gun" or high tech incapacitation device, a gentrification in law enforcement hiring practices seems to fall in lockstep with a push for technological solutions in apprehending violent offenders. While the advances in technology have definitely proven valuable in reducing the number of injuries for both officers and suspects, it also created images that generated a national and international calls for changes in police training and overall performance (Brooks 2020; Wood et al. 2020).

Putting aside the calls for police retraining, in light of the national and international demand, it is hoped that the current spate of violence and the spike in crime, including youth violence, will serve as a wake-up call to administrators and policy-makers that the training methods and hiring practices need to drastically change to address this as well as the de-escalation methods.

The growing incidence of youth violence and the near epidemic proportions of bloodshed in schools have forced agencies to prepare for the unthinkable. Most agencies have now undergone some form of active shooter training in an effort to respond to a student on a violent rampage. Yet, while the mechanics of clearing a building are being addressed, very little is being done to prepare the psyche for such an event.

Some officers are actually rebelling against their agencies when they have been forced to participate in Active Shooter training where officers who are first on the scene must form into a squad to go on the immediate offensive against the armed individuals who are actively shooting others, and where it is likely that the shooting will continue until the shooters are confronted. The officers justify their reluctance or outright refusal to participate by asserting that they never volunteered to be on a SWAT team, and that going on the offensive to hunt for someone who is actively killing people is not part of their job description.

There is an understandable repugnance toward the thought of shooting school-age children, but the hesitation to realistically train for this possibility because the concept is reprehensible will ultimately function as a handicap in the event that such skills become necessary.

Specialized training aside, many agencies cannot afford even the most basic training, let alone access to high tech training systems that can be used in-house for advanced training. For many agencies, there is basic training and then very little recurrent training. In the area of firearms training, an alarming number of agencies only participate in annual re-qualification, which is now broadly understood as not really training (Haberfeld 2018). Qualification is merely a demonstration that under controlled conditions, officers can demonstrate the basic mechanics of marksmanship proficiency.

The fragmentation of training that has occurred over the years is also quite troubling as the various use-of-force factions gang up against each other, disagreeing about the "right" technique or training philosophy. Defensive tactics (DT) and firearms instructors have rarely been on the same page when it comes to tactics, although this has been changing in recent years. The International Association of Law Enforcement Firearms Instructors (IALEFI) has migrated to the term "Use-of-Force Instructor," breaking it down further into areas of specialization. While this might seem like a fruitless exercise in semantics, it is actually a fundamental shift toward the recognition that all trainers involved in any use-of-force teaching must have an understanding of the other components (IALEFI 2020).

Other positive changes in training are beginning to emerge. Those involved in Reality-Based Training are reducing the use of negative reinforcement training, which is a good thing. Although this style of training is addressed at various places throughout this book, it has relevance here because it plays heavily into the conditioning process of a police officer or soldier. The concept of placing students in situations designed to provide them a negative training experience used to be so prevalent with some of the "gloom and doom" style instructors that many officers currently on the street have been over-sensitized to the "bad" that exists out there, making them risk aversive to the extent that they avoid high-risk situations.

The main problems with negative reinforcement or punishment are:

- Punished behavior is suppressed, not forgotten. Behavior can return when the punishment is no longer present. This means punishment for tactical error will not necessarily correct the behavior.
- Punishment causes increased aggression because it teaches that aggression is the way to cope with problems. This means that officers might overreact to situations and take actions that could be construed as excessive force.
- Punishment creates fear that can generalize to undesirable behavior, building in a broad level of anxiety to calls for service that are similar to the negative training experiences, resulting in the possible avoidance of high-risk calls.
- Punishment does not necessarily guide an individual toward desired behavior. Positive reinforcement indicates the kind of behavior that is desirable. Punishment only teaches what not to do.
- Punishment teaches how to avoid future punishment. Officers will often find ways to opt out of training that attempts to use punishment as a teaching tool, or it may create a reluctance in the real world to take potentially dangerous calls for service.

One form of potentially negative reinforcement training that is still widely used includes the presentation of videotaped incidents showing officers getting killed or injured.

This brief's authors believe that such videos are shown indiscriminately for the "shock value" in the same way that "killing" an officer in training scenarios has been inappropriately used to demonstrate the consequences of poor tactics. However, there might be some merit in using these recorded tragedies together with a Reality-Based Training program that insists on 100% performance to successfully complete the scenario. Inasmuch as it is permissible to "shoot" a student during a training scenario (if this is what has been scripted), provided that he/she is encouraged to stay in the fight, return fire, move to cover, and "survive" the encounter, the real-life videos can be used during an after action review to validate the necessity for decisive action and illustrate the consequences of poor tactics in the real world. It is also helpful if the video examples depict events similar to those encountered during the training scenario.

There are two major concerns about using the footage captured by the dash (Brooks 2020) and body worn cameras:

1. Dashcams are typically used to illustrate poor tactical choices. The initial danger in using them this way is the principle of "failing to educate," or what Dennis Waitley refers to as "motivating through the negative … don't." Do not show someone's failure over and over and expect them to have some sort of epiphany. Osmosis exists in areas other than cellular nutrition. Show your people warriors and the tactical superiority of the research in training, and you will see improvement in their abilities.
2. This brings us to the next paradox…. why are we not seeing classic "counters," accurate shooting, decisive verbal intervention, and so on? If what was being taught was realistic and effective, we would see more of it on the video cams. In reality, training is still quite robotic. It does not integrate researched behavioral realities; when it does, it is extremery rare and sporadic. The tactics are still being taught in a cooperative and somewhat robotic manner.

So what do we do with the dashcam and body worn camera footage? Can they be a valuable resource? Absolutely, but experience needs to be used as well to stimulate and educate. Using a dashboard or body worn camera video strips the deniability of poor performance from the student … this is real, it happened, and we are going to learn from it. That is the ultimate gift the participants can share—the lessons learned. However, lessons learned cannot simply be reminders or lip service, they must be lessons that cement their laws into our minds through physical repetition, so that we need not "remember" what to do, we know what to do.

References

Barrett, K. J., Haberfeld, M. M., & Walker, M. C. (2009). A comparative study of the attitudes of urban, suburban and rural police officers in New Jersey regarding the use of force. *Crime, Law and Social Change, 52*(2), 159–179.

Brooks, R. (2020). Stop training police like they're joining the military. *The Atlantic magazine.* https://www.theatlantic.com/ideas/archive/2020/06/police-academies-paramilitary/612859/. Retrieved July 25, 2020.

Crank, J. P. (2014). *Understanding police culture.* Routledge. https://blauerspear.com/. Retrieved on July 23, 2020.

Denef, S., Bayerl, P. S., & Kaptein, N. A. (2013, April). *Social media and the police: Tweeting practices of British police forces during the August 2011 riots*. In Proceedings of the SIGCHI conference on human factors in computing systems, pp. 3471–3480.

FBI Press Release. (2020). *2019 Statistics on law enforcement officers killed in the line of duty.* https://www.fbi.gov/news/pressrel/press-releases/fbi-releases-2019-statistics-on-law-enforcement-officers-killed-in-the-line-of-duty. Retreievd July 24, 2020.

Haberfeld, M. (2016). The triangle of recruitment, selection, and training in the 21st century policing. In M. Deflem (Ed.), *The politics of policing: Between force and legitimacy* (Sociology of Crime, Law, and Deviance) (Vol. 21, pp. 295–313). Bingley: Emerald.

Haberfeld, M. R. (2017). *Warrior of guardian or both? Effective counter terrorist tactics and olice integrity, to shoot or not to shoot: Is this the question?* Article published by the European Union Agency for Law Enforcement Training (CEPOL), Budapest, Hungary, 2017.

Haberfeld, M. R. (2018). *Critical issues in police training*. Pearson Custom Publishing.

Haberfeld, M. (2019). Who will stand up for the police? *The New York Daily News*. https://www.nydailynews.com/opinion/ny-oped-who-will-stand-up-for-police-20190724-khvha4nlcjf4dpgwpmoozvoxa4-story.html. Retrieved July 25, 2020.

Haberfeld, M. R., Lieberman, C. A., & Horning, A. (2015). *Introduction to policing; the pillar of democracy*. Carolina Academic Press.

International Association of Firearms Instructors. (2020). https://www.ialefi.com/. Retrieved July 25, 2020.

Levine, P. B., & McKnight, R. (2017). Firearms and accidental deaths: Evidence from the aftermath of the Sandy Hook school shooting. *Science, 358*(6368), 1324–1328.

Scottie, A. (2020). *There is a growing call to defund the police. Here's what it means.* CNN. https://www.cnn.com/2020/06/06/us/what-is-defund-police-trnd/index.html. Retrieved July 25, 2020.

Shultz, J. M., Muschert, G. W., Dingwall, A., & Cohen, A. M. (2013). The Sandy Hook Elementary School shooting as tipping point: "This time is different". *Disaster Health, 1*(2), 65–73.

The Baltimore Sun. (1995). *School bus is high-jacked, suspect slain: Disabled children used as shields in Florida chase.* https://www.baltimoresun.com/news/bs-xpm-1995-11-03-1995307039-story.html. Retrieved July 25, 2020.

Walker, M. C., Haberfeld, M. R., Horwitz, D., & Albert, C. (2011). *An investigation into the murders of law enforcement officers in the first 75 days of 2011 and those who committed the crimes*. New York: John Jay College of Criminal Justice. This study was funded by the Federal Bureau of Investigation, Law Enforcement Services Section.

Wood, G., Tyler, T., & Papachristos, A. V. (2020). *Procedural justice training reduces police use of force and complaints against officers*. https://www.pnas.org/content/117/18/9815. Retrieved July 25, 2020.

Chapter 6
The Mechanics of Reality-Based Training (RBT): The Delivery of the "Unconscious Competence"

This chapter, as well as the following Chap. 7, is based primarily on the personal, decades long experience of one of the authors of this brief, Ken Murray. As such, it is much more practical and tactical in nature. While we recognize the importance of proper refences of the materials presented in a peer-reviewed publication, this chapter is mostly a product of Mr. Murray's personal experience (Murray 1995–2020).

Reality-Based Training, Confrontational Simulation (Con-Sim), Scenario Training, Role Play, Use-of-Force Simulation Training, Video Simulation, Tactical Simulations, Force-on-Force, Op-For Training, Live Target Engagement, Field Problems, Mock Disasters, Experiential Training.

It goes by many names, but the premise of training remains the same. Place a student into a setting that simulates a real-life encounter to test his/her ability to respond to that incident while acting within departmental policy and the law. Sounds easy. It is not. If it is to be done properly, the training must be a highly structured, carefully designed situation with predictable outcomes and tightly structured roles and responsibilities for the training staff.

One of the key challenges for trainers who foray out into the world of RBT is that when properly implemented, RBT does not easily conform to many of the organizational norms currently associated with conventional styles of training. It will be necessary to recalibrate some of the beliefs held by individuals in the agency, as well as the agency as a collective, to evolve to the new training paradigm.

Changing individual beliefs is difficult, but changing an institutional belief system is hard! Students who have come through my instructor schools encounter resistance when they take the new information back to their agencies.

To achieve success with this program, you will need organizational will, sustained funding, clear and uninterruptible supply lines, reinforcements, and a belly-ful of determination. The first step is to suspend your own internal tendency to say, "They'll never allow me to do that …"

If you persevere long enough, and constantly take small steps toward change, change will occur. These small changes have a cumulative effect over time and

K. R. Murray, M. R. Haberfeld, *Use of Force Training in Law Enforcement*, SpringerBriefs in Criminology, https://doi.org/10.1007/978-3-030-59880-8_6

eventually create substantial change. Occasionally, windows of opportunity for substantial change will open. There might be a catastrophic event such as a lawsuit, a training tragedy, or a new legislation that mandates more realistic training. In certain situations in which police actions were deemed inappropriate, there have been instances where plaintiffs in lawsuits would waive compensation if training is undertaken to correct the problem that caused the tragedy. For example, in the wake of the accidental shooting of a 12-year-old hostage on the West Coast, the parents of the slain boy agreed not to seek monetary damages against the city if they improve their firearms training program.

Whatever creates the window of opportunity, it is important to be prepared to use it as a springboard for permanent change because as quickly as the window opened, it is just as likely to close back up. When the change does begin, keep it rolling and take pride in your accomplishments, since because of your efforts, there will be fewer officer-involved injuries, fewer questionable shootings, and fewer citizen complaints.

Getting a simulation program the support it needs is a tough sell for many agencies. Those who attended my instructor development programs were often sent there by the command staff—much as someone might send their errand boy to procure some aspirin for a headache. One of the problems with attending my school is that while running that "errand," many instructors discover deeply rooted, systemic problems with their departmental training policies. That "headache" turns out to be a "brain cancer" and substantial "surgery" is required to correct the problem. Some administrators, when faced with this revelation, will simply shrug and instruct their staff to just "buy stronger aspirin." It will stop the pain for a brief period, but does nothing to cure the underlying problem. Band-aid solutions for sucking chest wounds never work out in the long run, and it is frustrating for trainers who return from my training courses when they are not provided the resources by their agency to solve the problems they were originally sent to the school to solve!

How Training Is Currently Done Versus a More Effective Way

The current training paradigm for most types of training calls for relatively brief training sessions with high student-instructor ratios. This might work well for some topics such as legal updates or Human Diversity Refresher training, but it does not work well with Reality-Based Training. To be truly effective, a comprehensive RBT program must be done through block training, or alternatively, through a process known as on-duty/in-service training where the training sites are set up for a number of weeks and officers cycle through the sites during any downtime they may have during an active shift. On-duty/in-service training is very effective but untenable for some agencies given their high volume of calls for service.

Many agencies go out and buy all the gear, believing that they are now ready to jump right in to RBT. It is like buying a supercomputer without the operating system software. The big difference is that the computer will not kill you if you plug it in incorrectly.

The real problem lies in the fact that Reality-Based Training looks easy. Because of this, majority of agencies buy some of "simms" (sic) gear, grab a couple of guys to be role players, throw some officers into a few loosely structured situations, and see what they do. Most of the training staff have fun "killing off" the students, believing they are actually doing the students a favor by showing them how nasty the world can be. Then they report back to the administration that the program was successful. There is often little regard for the lurking dangers until someone gets injured, then everyone wags fingers at everyone else, searching for a scapegoat.

"Why do I have to go to school for a week to learn how to shoot paintballs at people?"

You do not. It is absolutely unnecessary to send a person to a school to teach them how to shoot paintballs.

Teaching people how to shoot paintballs is not what this training provides. In fact, there is not much in my 5-day RBT Instructor School. We shoot as much ammunition as is necessary to teach how to run a safe and realistic training. Our time together is dedicated to providing you the maximum amount of knowledge about Reality-Based Training as the time permits. All the necessary topics dealing with training ammunition and device usage, safety rules and standards, and protective equipment issues are thoroughly covered. Participants are taught how to run their own safe and effective comprehensive training programs, and to develop effective scenarios that are designed to directly connect their departmental use-of-force model with officer actions, while reducing injuries and liability exposure. The school is not product specific, but rather teaches training concepts through which you can make better use of whichever technologies you chose to use, although I do provide guidance as to the pros and cons of various types of popular training equipment and ammunition. Most of the topics covered in this book are covered in the 5-day instructor school.

Despite what some trainers would try to have you believe, you cannot safely learn how to run effective scenarios in 1 or 2 days. Even after 5-day schools, a lot of information is going to gel in the minds of the instructors, and part of the value of this book is to provide a ready reference to reinforce what was learned in class.

These courses include a significant classroom component that spends a great amount of time on issues covered in this book. It is not just about how to use some specific technology or simply how to set up a scenario. It is a blending of psychology, philosophy, and technology. It is a synergistic program that deals equally with the "down-range" effects the training will have on students when they are faced with real-world problems. Unlike other classes that are available elsewhere, my class endeavors to provide instructors not only "the how" and "the what" of Reality-Based Training, but also "the why." These are some of the major differences between my school and the other schools that purport to teach the concepts of Reality-Based Training.

"We've been doing this for years now. What can you possibly teach me?"

Trainers who have been using RBT for years routinely write on their comment cards that they came into the class because they were required to be there—sent there by their agency for liability reasons—and had no expectations of leaving with any additional information than what they arrived with. They thought they were coming to school to learn to properly use an equipment designed for Live Target Engagement (LTE.) At the completion of the program, most are surprised to discover how much is involved in running a safe and effective RBT, and are often amazed that they have not hurt anyone doing things the way they had been doing them in their own training programs.

"We don't have the time or the money to send anyone right now. We're too busy training people."

As for time and money, both are already spent. In the absence of a proper training program, an agency is either going to spend time and money in defending lawsuits, paying the added expense of workman's compensation claims, or absorbing lost man-hours because of unnecessary injuries. A properly structured Reality-Based Training has the potential to reduce the amount of money that is unnecessarily paid out in lawsuits by avoiding the situations that cause them.

Agencies that adopted a comprehensive RBT program have experienced a decline in officer-involved injuries as well as a reduction in complaints and lawsuits from citizens. If your agency is self-insured, as are most these days, ask your "Risk Manager" how much he/she assigns to a wayward bullet or excessive force claim, then add up those costs to your agency over the past 5 years. Some "risk managers" note that when all the costs are added in to a shooting, the cost per bullet fired is approximately 10,000 dollars, and that is if the bullet does not really hit anything of value. If it hits someone, the cost goes up to about 50,000 dollars, and that is if it is a justified shooting. For unjustified shootings or accidental death of a bystander, the sky is the limit with price tags in the range of millions of dollars. It is impossible to put a price tag on the tragic killing of an innocent bystander in the street or of an officer in training, but all the hearthache and loss aside, an accidental shooting during an RBT session on the West Coast cost the agency over 10 million dollars in punitive damages, and accidental shootings of innocent civilians routinely result in awards of millions of dollars.

If your program can stop just one or two wayward bullets from being launched on an annual basis through training your officers to respond more effectively and decisively, you will be able to easily pay for the costs of a program such as I describe. If you can avoid the cost of settling just one unfavorable excessive force or wrongful death lawsuit, you could probably fund Reality-Based Training programs for about a hundred agencies.

"We've had people hurt in 'that type' of training and we're not doing it anymore."

Hurting people during RBT to the extent that it caused the termination of the program indicates that the training was being done in a haphazard or frivolous manner. If you educate your staff to set the training up properly and allocate the necessary resources to do it right, most of the injuries will vanish along with the liability statistics.

Projectile-Based Training Considerations

Whenever a Non-Lethal Training Ammunition (NLTA) is used during Reality-Based Training, there are lots of opportunities for things to go wrong. The unintentional introduction of live weapons and ammunition has led to far too many injuries and deaths. On a lesser but still important scale, participants in training exercises utilizing NLTA have received permanent scars from projectile strikes with or without the use of protective gear. Surprisingly to many, psychological damage can also be inflicted. Projectile-based training is a veritable hornets nest, but there are plenty of good things that can come from using NLTA, if it is properly employed.

The three major considerations in using projectiles in a force-on-force training program are:

- The dangers of projectile-based Live Target Engagement
- The usefulness of pain penalties
- The usefulness of "paint" marks during Live Target Engagement

The Dangers of Projectile-Based Live Target Engagement

If you are going to use projectiles during your Reality-Based Training program, some welts and bruises are unavoidable. Part of the value of Live Target Engagement (LTE) is derived from the possibility of a "pain penalty" for tactical error. There is, however, a fine line between using the technology for teaching lessons and using it for frivolous punishment.

Frivolous punishment is not useful. It is a dangerous practice, it is guaranteed to create some terrible tissue trauma, and it can get an otherwise good training program shut down. Some people do not mind the welts and bruises. In fact, some groups think it is somehow "cool" to parade around their "war wounds" following a training session. They might even call other members within their agency "wussies" for not wanting to expose themselves to that type of peril. This type of "bonding" behavior, something culturally acceptable within various tightly knit communities inside the military and law enforcement circles, has actually gotten training programs shut down once administrators learn of the potential for "permanent disfigurement." Projectile-based training is much too valuable to have it shut down because of a few individuals that live by the adage "Wounds heal, pain is temporary, chicks dig scars, and glory is forever."

From a training perspective, a projectile strike is useful only to the extent that it can be used for corrective measures. One or two shots are usually sufficient. Unloading an entire magazine on someone is not. It is wasteful, dangerous, counterproductive, and ill-conceived. When I am running an exercise, my role players are typically armed only with revolvers for two reasons. First, revolvers are much more resilient and likely to endure the rigors of being constantly dropped on the ground during training. Second, it limits the number of rounds that a suspect can fire. Six is plenty during most scenarios for a role player. If the point cannot be made with six rounds, you probably need to change your scenario, your role player, or perhaps carefully evaluate the tactical capabilities of your student.

The difference between an effective use of projectiles during training and a frivolous free-for-all is similar to that of the difference between spanking your child and child abuse. One or two swats as a corrective measure usually make the point. A continuous beating is tantamount to a criminal act.

The Hodge-Podge of Doom

For those who argue that being the recipient of a large volume of fire desensitizes a participant to the act of being shot at, there are more effective ways to accomplish this without the resultant physical or psychological trauma. There is also the likelihood that a recipient of such a reckless bombardment will condition a flinch response or an aversion to future encounters where he/she might be shot at, rather than inoculate him/her to the experience. I submit for your consideration that those who profess that there is a great deal of training value in shooting vast numbers of projectiles at their students are more interested in playing paintball than they are in conditioning useful survival skills.

The Usefulness of Pain Penalties

It is important to understand the psychology through which a pain penalty works in this type of training. The underlying premise is that an irrational fear can cause predictable behaviors that can be leveraged to extract better training value. Fear is irrational because the behavior many people demonstrate in response to the possibility of getting whacked with a projectile is often well out of proportion to the actual event. Getting hit with a paintball stings, but it is really not that bad. If it were, there would not be a multi-million dollar industry built around it. The anxiety generated by the anticipation of the pain is more useful for training purposes than the actual experience of the pain itself. In other words, for behavior modification purposes, a threatened pain event is often more effective than an actual pain event.

By way of an example, let us use the common bee sting. . Bee stings hurt, but they are not devastating unless you happen to have an allergy to bee venom. Although for most people, a bee sting is a painful reminder of why we should not antagonize bees. Many people are so afraid of bees that they experience anxiety in the casual presence of a single bee. Some have actually run their vehicles off the road if a bee happened to be sucked in a window. Had the bee actually stung them, which is quite unlikely to happen, the consequences of that sting would have been far less than the consequences of smashing their cars.

It is the same with a pain penalty during Live Target Engagement. Many participants have an irrational fear about the possibility of being hit with a projectile, and that fear raises stress levels to the point where their conscious resources are fully occupied with pain avoidance. As discovered in Chap. 2, if the conscious mind is occupied or the sympathetic nervous system is activated, a person will only have access to those skills that have been conditioned to the Unconscious Competence level. Any attempt by the student to use skills not conditioned to this level will often fail, thereby providing the Exercise Controller with important insight into the student's ability to face a critical incident.

The concept of a pain penalty will only be useful in helping the training staff to observe technical and tactical deficiencies if:

- The scenario is sufficiently realistic to fully engage the student as if it were an actual event.
- The student actually exhibits adaptive behaviors consistent with pain avoidance.
- The Exercise Controller is completely focused on the actions of the student to observe the telltale deficiencies, indicating that the skills necessary to solve the problem have not been conditioned to the Unconscious Competence level.

If these conditions do not exist, then the pain penalty is not useful. In fact, it simply adds unnecessary hazard to the training environment. Putting too much padding on a student to completely eliminate the possibility of a pain penalty nullifies the usefulness of projectiles in training, since students eventually realize that they are not going to feel anything if they get hit, so they are no longer risk aversive. It is like putting someone in a shark cage. After the first couple of adrenaline rushes before you completely learn to trust the protective ability of the cage, you become complacent knowing that you cannot be injured while inside it.

Training technologies that have been shown to be useful in creating an "aversion response" from students during LTE include various brands of marking projectiles, solid plastic projectiles (AirSoft pellets, not the cartridges that fall under the USTA category), wax projectiles, cotton wads, and certain electronic devices.

No one gets out of the scenarios without complete demonstration of all the performance activities necessary to complete the performance objective. In the real world, there is only one determining criterion of success in combat, and that is whether an adversary is capable of continuing hostile action. There is no magic number of projectile hits, and there are very few mystical locations that will reliably put down a hostile subject. This is where conventional firearms training and many training simulators often fall short of providing effective training. They treat participants like scoreboards and often base the "win" or the "loss" on factors that may or may not be the key determinant of winning a real-world encounter. When it comes to using lethal force, to my mind, it is much more important that a student in my scenarios focuses on the problem of putting his/her adversary down and keeping him/her down. Students are not allowed to stop thinking or stop fighting until the Safety Officer ends the scenario. This will condition a "winning mindset." This type of training requires a great deal of expertise and dedication on the part of the training staff to stay focused on this goal, and a great deal of education and practice in learning how to develop and run a program that fulfills this objective.

The Usefulness of Marks During Live Target Engagement

There are several different technologies available for use in NLTA exercises. Some trainers have chosen to use conventional paintball guns in their training programs for cost reasons. Conventional paintball guns function differently than duty weapons and can unintentionally condition incorrect weapon handling. For students, I believe it is critical that they use the same model of firearm for training as that which they carry on duty, although this is not necessarily so for the role player. Using actual firearms that have been converted for use with NLTA is useful, but not essential. Other emerging technologies such as AirSoft pistols are gaining a great deal of popularity among trainers. Their realistic look, feel, and function make them very effective during Reality-Based Training. They fire 6mm plastic BBs at a respectable velocity—certainly enough to create that "pain penalty" risk aversion. The only downside for many trainers is the lack of a mark. Some of the suppliers for AirSoft equipment have developed 6mm marking projectiles, although from my own tests I do not believe that the reliability, durability, feeding, or projectile breakage is quite good enough for the military and law enforcement training just yet. Perhaps someday it will be.

When it comes to force-on-force Reality-Based Training, what some trainers need to realize is that although marking projectiles are useful to a certain extent, you do not always need a mark, and if costs are an issue, you might want to consider whether or not you do.

Keeping your eyes on the world of technology is essential, since there is always some new gadget making its way to the RBT equipment arena. Blank guns and AirSoft weapons are often neglected by trainers because they do not leave a mark, and some trainers believe that in the absence of a mark there will be arguments between students and role players as to whether they "got" each other. We are not 10-year-olds anymore playing cops and robbers. I hope I never hear anyone in a serious training exercise arguing "I got you" … "No you didn't!" Even without input from the Exercise Controller, a role player should be able to decide by watching the student when he/she [the role player] has been hit. Whether or not marking cartridges are being used, it is unlikely that the role player will even feel the hits or be able to see the marks anyway, so he/she must be trained to observe the student as well as watch or listen for cues from the Exercise Controller to know when he/she is supposed to begin going down.

One of the downsides of marking cartridges that very few trainers consider is that many students start to condition themselves to look for the hit, or the "hole" that they made on a role player, rather than continuously responding to his/her actions until he/she is down. There are many times in an actual gunfight where you will not see the bullet holes in a suspect, nor any blood spurting from him/her. If a student

c   o   n   d   i   t   i   o   n   s
him/her self to believe that seeing the physical effects from the impact of his bullets is the only measure of effective gunfire, he/she might start psyching him/her self out, believing that the recipient of his/her gunfire is somehow indestructible. Remember, the marks made by some types of NLTA are useful to a certain point, but they are not absolutely essential and are often overrated. In fact, many of the marking projectiles that are currently available do not really mark all that well, and may not even mark at all in the event of a glancing blow or if the participants are wearing certain types of clothing. If you have built some sort of "scoring" system around a "paint check" as they do in a paintball game, what then?

Moreover, although there is exceptional value in shooting projectiles at students if properly and professionally utilized (due primarily to the training value of the pain penalty discussed earlier), there is absolutely no value in having a pain penalty for the role player. Because of this, it raises some interesting training questions.

Benefits

- Permits after action review of a student's shooting performance on the suspect
- Demonstrates where "missed" projectiles have struck
- Allows for discrimination between multiple shooters
- High interest among users
- Realistic functioning of firearms

Detriments

- Costly
- Potential for physical injury, especially with role players
- Requirement of "projectile-friendly" environment
- Necessity of protective equipment that restricts realistic facial expressions, casualty simulation, etc.
- Often leads to "paintball mentality" during training

As you can see, there is a balance between the benefits and detriments of shooting projectiles at role players. While it obviously has some value, it might be worthwhile to begin thinking about the future of training and some of the realism that could be achieved by eliminating the detriments associated with projectile-based training. This might be accomplished through a mixture of training technologies, but the solution cannot possibly be simply technological in nature. First, improving realism would most certainly require a higher degree of training for role players to get them to act extremely realistically, despite the fact that there is nothing being shot at them. Second, it will also require a higher degree of professionalism on the part of the students, since many would complain about not getting to actually shoot projectiles at the role player. Many would raise an issue of fairness, suggesting that it is not fair for the role player to be able to shoot projectiles at them without being able to shoot something back. Much of this attitude boils down to the gamesmanship that many students still bring with them to the training, where they apply the rules of "paintball," either consciously or subconsciously, to the professional Reality-Based Training environment. Third, there would have to be a substantial improvement in the training of the Exercise Controllers to interact with both the student and the role player to extract a higher level of information from the actions of the student. Fourth, the scenarios themselves would have to be written much better than what is often currently being done.

The Necessity for Identical Equipment Manipulation

There are several dedicated paintball guns which are the same size and shape of several popular pistol and sub-machinegun patterns. The supplier of one of the better devices I have seen is Asia Paintball Supply that manufactures the Real Action Markers. These training weapons show promise for use in some of the lower levels of RBT, but because reloading and malfunction clearing on these training devices is different than on actual weapons, caution is urged on how they are used in training. It is necessary to utilize training devices that require identical manipulation especially in high-stress areas such as reloading and malfunction clearing.

To that end, for training where skills are being built and integrated under stress, it is recommended that trainers stick with AirSoft guns or the specialized marking cartridges that fit in actual firearms that have been converted for use with NLTA. This ensures that all weapon manipulations by the student—from reloads to malfunctions—are identical to that of their actual weapon. Changing the way you perform any of these critical skills can condition improper techniques, which could ultimately spell disaster in a crisis. For example, people have been killed when they have been trapped inside a strange car where the door handles function slightly different from the car they normally ride in. Skydivers have been killed after borrowing a gear where the deployment system is slightly different. There are basically three places where your deployment device will sit on your parachute … on your leg, on the bottom of the parachute container, or near the opening flap of the container. Although it sounds reasonable to assume that if you feel around in one place and the deployment device is not there, you would simply remember that you are wearing a borrowed equipment and reach to the other spot for the deployment device. Unfortunately, this is not the way the brain works in a critical situation, and experienced skydivers have been killed as a result. A similar failure might occur if critical weapon manipulations are different in training than they are in the real world.

If you are using training devices where you have to do things differently when performing fine or complex motor skills, you are programming incorrect torque profiles, which under stress, could set in motion a chain of events from which it might be difficult to recover. Reloading techniques, the manipulation of de-cockers, and the ability to clear malfunctions are critical lifesaving skills that should be conditioned at the Unconscious Competence level, and training in those skills should be accomplished using either the actual weapon you will be using or an identical training version.

Learn to Accept and Channel the Effects of Stress

Reality-Based Training provides the framework for students to receive the "stress inoculation" that Dave Grossman talks about. Knowing what the physiological effects may be in advance of a stressful encounter and having the awareness to recognize the physical manifestations of stress when they are occurring provide officers with information that can mean the difference between living and dying. But simply knowing about those effects is not enough—many must be experienced.

Preparing your students for the reality of the streets is one of the most rewarding tasks of being a Reality-Based Trainer. When building basic skills, it is necessary to keep the level of induced stress to a lower level, but once basic skills have been mastered and combinations of skills are smooth, then training must be sufficiently engaging to cause a stress response so that you, the trainer, can address any inappropriate responses during the training as well as during the debriefing at the conclusion of the training session. The drills start out slowly and build progressively to higher and higher degrees of speed, aggression, and stress.

During High-Level Scenarios, where both the knowledge and tactical abilities of a student are being tested "in context," it is important to create a sufficiently stressful situation to provide the student with the experience of physiological and emotional arousal, and ensure that he/she has the tools and techniques to work through and overcome the negative effects of stress. It is therefore essential to make certain that he/she emerges from that encounter a winner. By doing these things, you help program into your student solid survival skills that will be available to him/her during the most decisive moments of his/her life. There is no greater gift that you can give to your student than for him/her to return to his/her loved ones no matter how bad his/her day was.

3. **Train Officers to Win**

- Do not give it away.
- Stop "killing" your students in training.
- The problem with negative reinforcement training.

Do Not Give It Away

Training officers to win does not mean having a role player give up unrealistically during a High-Level Scenario or letting sub-standard officers pass through the gauntlet just because they showed up. Training an officer to win means not letting a scenario to end until he/she prevails, and also avoiding the use of "no-win" scenarios.

The object of Reality-Based Training is to develop an officer's ability to respond to critical and life-threatening encounters by basing future responses on past successful experiences.

I have seen a lot of RBT where the staff makes it extremely difficult, if not impossible, for an officer to complete a scenario successfully. This is a direct result of poorly selected or untrained role players, badly designed scenarios, lack of training preparation on the part of the training staff, or unclear training objectives. Add to this the tendency of trainers to stop a scenario immediately after the shots are fired, and officers are being unnecessarily deprived of positive training experiences. The section dealing with immediate remediation later on in this chapter describes in detail the method for taking officers through a much more effective experience.

Giving your students the experience of "death" during a simulation exercise teaches them to die, not live, and this is not an effective way to teach people to survive.

It is my unwavering position that every student emerging from a scenario comes out a winner.

What is meant by ensuring that a student emerges from an encounter a winner is this: a student must win either through superior tactics or sheer perseverance. They might get shot during the scenario; they might get stabbed; they might get beaten to the ground—all of this is fair play if that is what has been written into your scenario. However, when any of these events occur, the scenario does not end. In fact, it might be necessary to intervene if the student tries to quit or if there is a true safety concern, but this does not mean that the scenario is over. It does not end until the student does something that can contribute to his/her own survival, after which it continues until it reaches one of the three "natural conclusions" presented later in this chapter.

For example, if during a High-Level Scenario, the student missed all the pre-attack cues from the role player and ends up getting shot, the Exercise Controller must make certain that the scenario continues until the student returns effective fire, gets to a position of advantage, and calls for backup and EMS. Many students will want to quit on you … they have often been pre-conditioned either by earlier RBT, some simulators, paintball wars, or even television. They believe that when the rounds impact on them they are "out" or "dead." It is important that you break this dangerous conditioned response and replace it with a survival response.

Stop "Killing" Your Students in Training

The purpose of this section is to make the initial point:

Stop "killing" your students in training!

Trainers will often find it difficult to break the habit of declaring people "dead" or "out" when they are hit. Even if you do not officially call them "dead" but rather rule them "out" or tell them to "take a knee," you are possibly programming a potentially self-destructive behavior that can replicate itself in the stress of an actual gunfight. During one of my instructor classes, I had a trainer from a Midwest department say that during the training with his tactical team he would make his tactical officers "go down" if they received a "non-survivable hit." Of course I had to ask what a non-survivable hit was. The trainer explained that a shot to the visor of the head armor would be registered as an immediate "kill" to the officer. I took issue with this and turned it into a roundtable discussion on the lethality of head wounds. It was the overwhelming experience of the participants that many of the officers there had first-hand experience with someone who had been shot in the head or had received other non-survivable wounds, yet continued to fight and even occasionally survived. During the FBI shootout in Miami, Platt and Matix (Thorton 1986) continued to fire lethal shots at the agents despite receiving actual non-survivable wounds. The training that Platt and Matix received never taught them to "go down" when hit.

An off-duty officer in California was shot square in the chest from point-blank range by a 14-year-old gang member armed with a 0.357. The bullet went through the front ribs and fragmented, nicking the stomach, liver, intestines, cut some arteries and veins, shattered the spleen, and hit the diaphragm. The main part of the bullet passed through the base of the heart and cracked another rib on its way out. The officer managed to return fire, then chase down the assailant and shoot him four times, killing him at the scene.

The trainers that "kill" their students in training are not doing it out of defective intention; it is their methodology of achieving their intended objective that is flawed. The objective of these trainers is ultimately to improve the survival skills of their officers. They have just never been told that their methodology is outdated. Once they have "seen the light," such trainers are usually the biggest fans of the proper way to instill these survival behaviors in their students. The trainer who makes his guys "go down" if they had received a "non-survivable hit" had a valuable training purpose in mind, but he did not have a skill set to achieve a more effective outcome at the time. His situation provides an excellent example of a well-intentioned trainer implementing what he thought was a useful exercise with the intention of improving the training for his unit. The only thing he failed to recognize was that he was programming some of his guys for failure if they were to get shot during an entry. What he was trying to accomplish with this exercise was to teach the team how to persevere in the event a team member does go down. He believed it would improve overall team capabilities in the event they had an officer go down for any reason during an entry. His goal was noble, and once the error of his ways was pointed out to him and a better way to achieve his goal was described, he had his "Ah-ha!" breakthrough and been doing things differently ever since.

Dealing with a down officer is an important requirement for teams to work through, but the same training result can be accomplished without the negative training effects. I recommend using one of the team members, temporarily recruited by the Exercise Controller, to act as a role player. This can be done with or without the rest of the team's knowledge. It is usually useful to initially practice this type of drill using the Low-Level Scenario model so that the team builds the necessary skills associated with such a complex problem.

Just before the scenario, the Exercise Controller can get together with one of the team members and "designate" him as a "casualty." At some point during the entry, the "casualty' will go down as the result of some scripted incident. It can be through being shot by the role player, stumbling and falling, etc. The team will then have to deal with the reality that this team member is down and must be evacuated.

This method is very different from programming an officer to go down when he/she is shot, since the team member now adopts the psychology that he/she is now one of the other role players, instead of conditioning him\her self to "go down when you're hit" in response to a hostile fire. There has not been any measurable detriment to officer performance in street situations from having been a role player where he/she always ends up going down when shot. Conditioning the expectation that he/she is supposed to go down as a role player seems to pre-code the psyche that the situation is not real, and does not result in a connection within the mid-brain between being shot and going down. This is also one of the reasons that I suggest that role players should only go down in response to the direction of the Exercise Controller rather than in response to being hit by a simulated gunfire. This creates an important distinction between officers and role players, and it might very well make the difference between winning and losing a battle during an actual lethal force encounter. Never condition your officers to go down in response to a hostile fire.

Not permitting a student to "die" during a training scenario does not mean that there are no consequences to his\her tactical errors. If a student is not responding correctly to a lethal threat, then it is permissible for the role player to administer a "consequence" to that error by shooting the officer. This should get the officer into the gunfight. If it does not, it might necessitate an intervention, as described a bit later in this chapter, since an officer may be experiencing a meltdown. I never tell an officer that he/she is dead. If he/she is shot, he/she must keep fighting until he/she wins. Telling an officer he/she is "dead" with the intent of teaching him/her how to live is a contradiction. It is a version of what behavioral psychologists call "negative reinforcement."

The Problem with Negative Reinforcement Training

If you begin to understand the psychological processes associated with negative reinforcement training, it makes sense that negative training is an extremely inefficient way to attempt to program a specific response.

For example, don't think of an orange elephant. Don't do it. Banish the thought of an orange elephant from your mind.

To "not think" of an orange elephant, you had to go inside your mind and make a representation of an orange elephant just for that instruction to make sense. Then you had to put a big "X" through it and try to banish it from your thought process. This in turn triggered an internal dialogue about having to refocus your conscious attention on something other than the orange elephant that made you think of that elephant again.

To help program future success in any endeavor, why not just focus on the things you want to focus on instead of telling someone what not to focus on. This may be easier said than done. All the way through grade school and into adulthood we have been taught what to do by being told what not to do. Consequently, we often chastise ourselves for foolish behavior and dwell on the negative rather than moving toward the positive. How many times have you heard someone giving instructions to someone else, phrasing it in a negative form?

- Don't be late.
- You're gonna cut yourself with that knife.
- Don't forget to pick up milk.

All the above statements have a dominant thought that is the opposite of the desired result. To get past each dominant thought, you have to negate the negative to get to the positive. It is much more neurologically efficient to state your request in positive terms, such as:

- Be home early.
- Be careful with the knife.
- Remember, we need milk.

Each of the second set of statements is expressed in positive terms, clearly indicating the desired outcome. Simply stated:

Never try to motivate anyone with the reverse of an idea!

It is much more effective to make positive statements. Forget the unsuccessful attempts. Focus instead on successes. This is not only useful during law enforcement training, but also when communicating with your kids, spouse, colleagues, or anyone else for that matter. Negative motivation is a bad habit. Break it, and experience the power of positive or motivating statements. It will take a lot of practice and self-awareness to overcome the tendency to motivate with the reverse of an idea or a negative statement, but it is worth the effort.

The next thing we need to do is to make the officers finish every scenario. Meaning, a scenario is never successfully concluded until the officer completes all the written performance activities, and ultimately, the performance objective.

There will be times when scenarios must be concluded for safety reasons, times when they may be paused for administrative reasons, and times when they should be ended because they have reached their natural conclusions. However, whether a scenario is stopped or paused should be a predictable event based on defined rules. These pause or termination points can be grouped into three or the "Rules of Three." These rule groups include:

- The natural conclusions to a scenario
- The intervention points and intervention questions during a scenario
- The unnatural conclusions to a scenario

Natural Conclusions to a Scenario

A natural conclusion is defined as the appropriate ending point of a scenario once the student has met the pre-determined performance objective.

To achieve maximum training benefit from a scenario, it must continue to the point of a natural conclusion. Unfortunately, many trainers stop the action immediately following any shooting that occurs, thereby missing an opportunity to observe any unsafe behaviors that often occur at a point after the shots were fired.

The primary reason many trainers stop the scenarios immediately after a shooting is that they believe "Our guys know what to do after a shooting. We ask them and they tell us."

I used to believe exactly the same, thinking that the shooting itself was the important part of the scenario with everything else being a waste of training time. How wrong I was!

The interesting thing is, within a very short period following a shooting during a scenario, the vast majority of students would be able to accurately "check list" or verbally describe all the things they would do following the shooting. The shots would be fired, the suspect would be down, the whistle would blow, and the student would take a few breaths to get centered. After a few moments of reflection, he/she would launch into an explanation of "what next." Imagine my surprise when I started letting scenarios continue to run long after the shots were fired. Students who "knew better" would start doing the strangest things, and it took a substantial degree of research and testing to begin to understand why.

During critical or life-threatening situations, if the student does not have experience upon which to draw or has not connected all the various experiences necessary to overcome a complex problem through simulation or a similar previous successful experience, the actions or reactions to such an event may not be sufficient to overcome the problem. Throw in the effects of the brain chemistry associated with the shock and after-shock of acute stress and it all makes sense.

But do not take my word for it. For you trainers who stopped a scenario after the bullets flew and then proceeded to ask the student what he/she would do next, I am sure you have found that many students come up with a tactically sound answer after a sufficient period of recovery and introspection. If this has been your experience, I challenge you to allow the scenario to continue beyond this point. Force the student to continue after the shots were fired and carefully watch what happens. Do they seek cover? Do they immediately approach the suspect? Do they reload? Do they call for assistance? You are likely to experience that many students who would normally be able to explain the correct "next steps" will often violate both departmental policy and officer safety principles if the scenario is allowed to continue, and most of those students will not be able to explain why. This is the value of continuing a scenario to its natural conclusion.

The three natural conclusions to a scenario are:

- The situation is under control, the problem is resolved, the subject leaves, and no one goes to jail.
- The suspect is in custody.
- The suspect has been shot and the officer maintains a position of advantage and is waiting for help.

Any conclusions other than these three constitute an incomplete scenario especially if the outcome requires a lethal force option.

The Situation Is Under Control

This is the most confusing for Reality-Based Training participants. Early adopters of Reality-Based Training had a tendency to write every scenario to be a "shoot" scenario. As such, most people who enter into the Reality-Based Training environment have an expectation that they are going to have to use their firearm. This predisposition interferes with effective training since participants are usually keyed up waiting for the "draw and fire" signal from the role player.

In a comprehensive Reality-Based Training program, we must break this cycle and recalibrate this expectation. When effectively done, the majority of scenarios utilized in a comprehensive training program are "no-shoot" scenarios. Once the students begin to become accustomed to this style of training, they will begin to relax into more realistic behavior patterns consistent with how they would approach real situations on the street. They must accept that even during scenarios, they can resolve situations using officer presence, negotiation, and problem-solving skills in addition to higher levels of force. Training staff can then observe students' abilities to function within the complete use-of-force model rather than simply watching them get into shoot-outs.

Suspect Is in Custody

This requires the use of various levels of force including, but not limited to, lethal force. The scenario does not end until the actions of the suspect have been completely controlled and any aggressive action is neutralized.

When the natural conclusion is "The suspect is in custody," it is often sufficient that the suspect has been placed in a position of disadvantage and is ready to be physically taken into custody. Unless the scenario has been written to test things such as a student's ability to search a suspect or his/her handcuffing procedures, you will find that a scenario can usually be concluded just before physical contact with a controlled suspect.

One of the most dangerous times for both the student and the role player is during the custody phase, so it is important to write into the scenario script whether there is likely to be a physical encounter. If this is not done, injury to a role player can often occur faster than an Exercise Controller can intervene to stop it.

Let us assume that your scenario has been written so that the role player is going to be compliant at a certain point. During the handcuffing phase, the student feels what he/she believes to be "resistance" from the role player. This "resistance" is merely the inflexibility of the role player because of the restrictions of the protective equipment. The student is all keyed up because of the earlier goings-on in the scenario and is still experiencing a bit of an adrenalin pump. To overcome the "resistance," the student drops a knee into the back of the role player and then cranks his/her arm a little too much, causing the role player to actually begin resisting in response to the pain. This ups the ante of the student who now finds him/her self in a physical confrontation with the role player—for real. The student, unaware that the dynamics of this encounter have changed from training to reality, continues to exert and even increase the pressure. The fight is on and people can get hurt, especially if the student is not wearing a protective suit. All this could have been avoided by simply ending the scenario before the hands-on portion.

Aggressive resistance from the role player is not even needed for injuries to occur. During a TASER® school on the East Coast, a student suffered a broken leg when a role player moved around in an effort to provide a low level of resistance. The students in TASER® classes are often concerned about the TASER® wires when they are making an approach to handcuff or otherwise control the suspect. Once they have had a bit of experience, it no longer becomes an issue. In this instance, the student moved in to handcuff the role player, and the role player rolled to one side, trapping the foot of the student. The continued motion resulted in a "freak" accident, and the student suffered a broken leg. There are three issues here. First, if the training point is simply to demonstrate that the wire is a non-issue during movement to closure, then the role player should remain completely still. Second, there was no necessity that actual handcuffing must occur to achieve the goal of this exercise, so the scenario perhaps continued beyond the completion of the performance objective, which is one of the leading contributors to injuries. Third, it would be possible to complete this exercise in a dynamic fashion if desired, but both the student and the role player should be wearing protective gear, which would have likely prevented the injury.

The most dangerous time for both the student and role player is the point of physical contact. It is essential to know exactly what it is that you are testing with the scenario, which will determine whether there is a necessity for role player movements or hard physical contact. If there is going to be a physical encounter, it should be a predictable event. Role players must be well-protected with sufficient quantity and quality of protective equipment to prevent injury from the responses that are likely to come from a student. Ideally, the student should always be wearing protective equipment to allow him/her to get into a physical encounter that approaches the level of a real fight. To do this, it is essential that the protective equipment have both the structural integrity and the flexibility to permit relatively unrestricted movement.

If the scenario is designed so that the likely response from a student is going to be a hands-on physical intervention, the role player must be physically protected as well as be the "right guy" for full contact fighting. Using the wrong person for that type of role play is guaranteed to result in injured officers and role players, since a role player who is not a trained fighter in good physical condition is going to over or under react, move wrong, or provide the wrong level of resistance. Injuries during this type of training are, for the most part, predictable and preventable through proper structuring of the scenario, proper issuance of protective equipment, and proper selection of the role player.

Inexperienced role players have also been injured after seeing an opportunity to "teach a student a lesson" after observing his/her lax tactics. This has resulted in an unplanned full-on physical confrontation between a student and a role player. Students, who are often keyed up to begin with, can respond to a role player's surprise actions with full power retaliation. Role players who have made an unscripted decision to attempt to disarm a student, for instance, have found themselves bleeding and hospitalized. In an effort to reduce the potential of physical danger, a role player must be taught to be completely compliant during any physical contact with the student, unless:

- She/he is properly protected using appropriate protective equipment.
- Her/his non-compliance has been scripted into the scenario.
- She/he has the skills and flexibility to avoid injury during physical confrontations.
- The Exercise Controller is fully aware of when the confrontation is likely to occur so he can be close enough to physically intervene if possible to avoid serious injuries.

For times when full handcuffing is not necessary to complete the performance objective, it is appropriate for the Exercise Controller to intervene just before physical contact between the student and the role player. The most effective method I have found is to touch the student on the shoulder, which is my signal to both the student and the role player that we are pausing the scenario, and ask, "What are you thinking?" The student will often respond that he/she is going to cuff and search the suspect.

Essentially, no critical incident in law enforcement is ever really over until the suspect has been completely controlled, which usually means he/she is dead, dying, or in handcuffs. It is also true that many suspects only begin to actively resist after the first handcuff is applied. Officer safety protocol suggests that we should ideally only be handcuffing someone who is compliant. Whether that means the suspect was talked, fought, tased, or shot into compliance is not the issue. Handcuffing, especially with actively resistive suspects, is also often done in the presence and assistance of additional officers.

The decision to not take a scenario all the way to full handcuffing is made for administrative and safety reasons. Training to the extent of full cuffing requires superior quality protective gear and very well-trained staff. This is pretty advanced matter, but given the recent high profile case, handcuffing of resisting suspects shoud be incorported into training (Booker, 2020).

No matter what type of RBT you choose to use, it is often a trade-off, but even so, it is still light years ahead of the types of training that have been prevalent in the past. RBT is not a substitute for actual real-world experience where someone is actually trying to do you harm, but it is a valuable training tool that will definitely prepare you for those real-world encounters if done safely and correctly. The proposed natural conclusions have been developed to provide an excellent balance between safety and realism.

The Suspect Has Been Shot

Range training can condition some dangerous beliefs and behaviors. One in particular is what a target will actually do after being hit by a gunfire. On a range with steel targets, it usually falls down. In a standard course of fire, a target is often considered neutralized after a prescribed number of hits or when it turns on its edge. On video simulators and many role plays, the scenario stops after the gunshots. This type of programming can cause problems when an officer gets into an actual shooting because it often conditions an expectation that the fight is over immediately after the rounds are placed on the target.

To overcome this, I teach role players to react more realistically to a gunfire. The Exercise Controller is in charge of signaling the role player when he is to go down, and when he goes down, he should be scripted to go down slowly and continue to pose a threat for a short period. This teaches officers to react to the threat, instead of firing a prescribed number of rounds with an expectation that the threat will be immediately neutralized. Unless a suspect receives sufficient trauma to the brain or spinal cord, he/she can still continue to fight. Even with a devastating heart shot or severed aorta, there is still a sufficient amount of oxygen in his/her brain to permit the suspect to continue to fight for 10–15 seconds. That is enough time for two or three typical police gunfights. This is why role players must be taught to respond more realistically instead of dropping like a sock monkey as soon as they are hit. When students are initially exposed to this type of training, many fall back into old range habits where they fire a few rounds and then stop. When the role player does not go down immediately after being hit by their simulated gunfire, the student will often cry foul, stating "I got him … he's dead!" They will, however, quickly acclimate to the "new rules" and rapidly learn to stay in the fight until it is actually over.

Many officers during Reality-Based Training will actually stop fighting after they have been shot or after they have shot the role player. All their training has conditioned them to quit after the shots have been fired. Unfortunately in the real world, this behavior can prove disastrous for an officer conditioned to do this.

The Intervention Guidelines

An intervention is different from "stopping" a scenario. While scenarios can be stopped for a variety of safety or administrative reasons, an intervention is very similar to pressing the "pause" button on the video machine so that you can take a little break from the action. Interventions provide the Exercise Controller the opportunity to "tweak" the brain of the student in an attempt to achieve a higher degree of conditioning and program a successful response in the future. This is one potential place that the "out of role" command could be effectively used … it pauses the scenario without necessarily ending the scenario.

Interventions must be used under specific circumstances and coordinated between the Exercise Controller and the role player. If the Exercise Controller and the role player have been trained to function as a team, the role player will notice when the Exercise Controller moves toward the student and touches him/her on the shoulder, or hear the phrase "out of role." These are the "pause" cues for the role player, and he must immediately cease his actions and wait for the Exercise Controller to step away from the student, thereby cuing him/her to continue.

The Intervention Points During a Scenario

The following explains "when" to intervene—the three intervention points—and then "how" to intervene—the three intervention questions—so that the student obtains the maximum benefit from the intervention.

The three intervention points for the Exercise Controller are:

- Unnatural pause
- Goofy Loop
- Meltdown

Unnatural Pause

This occurs during a scenario when a student becomes "stuck" and progress has stopped. It is recognizable by the fact that nothing is really happening, to the extent that the Exercise Controller can do a leisurely count from one to ten. Unnatural pauses occur when the student does not know what to do next or may mistakenly believe that the scenario is concluded. An astute Exercise Controller should be able to pick up some of the student's non-verbal communication cues as well, such as:

- Rocking
- Pacing
- Erratic hand movements
- Self-touching

These non-verbal cues often indicate a lack of rational problem-solving. It would be useful to have a "branch" in the scenario, or at the very least a programmed response to the unnatural pause phenomenon since this type of behavior is very common with inexperienced officers or officers who possess limited survival skills, regardless of their length of service.

Although role players must also recognize an unnatural pause, they must resist the natural temptation to try to "fill" it with improvised dialogue, since this will simply waste time and can often take the scenario in an unintended direction.

In the absence of a branch or programmed role player response in the scenario, the preferred method for dislodging a "stuck" student is the use of Socratic Questioning. If the student intellectually knows what to do next, this technique will get his/her actions back on track. If he/she has stopped because he/she has decided for him/her self that the scenario is over, through your questioning process, you will quickly find out why he/she thinks it is over.

Remember—there are only three acceptable natural conclusions to a scenario:

- The situation is under control, the problem is resolved, the subject leaves, and no one goes to jail.
- The suspect is in custody.
- The suspect has been shot and the officer maintains a position of advantage and is waiting for help.

In an unnatural pause situation, determine if one of these situations has been reached. If it has not, the scenario must continue. It is up to the student to bring the scenario to one of these conclusions, and in the absence of his/her own initiative some gentle prodding may be necessary. The specific phrases that are helpful in moving things along will be covered shortly under the Three Questions for Interventions.

Goofy Loop

It has been said that a definition of insanity is doing the same thing over and over and expecting a different result. So it goes with the second intervention point, called the Goofy Loop:

Drop the gun, put it down, drop the weapon, I'm not telling you again, drop it, drop it now, sir ... drop ... the ... gun, DROP the gun, DROP THE GUN ...

If you hear your student constantly repeats the same thing or versions of the same thing, or you observe him/her unsuccessfully attempts the same action three or more times, you are witnessing a Goofy Loop. He/she is stuck and needs to be dislodged. You must have a branch in the scenario for such an occurrence or utilize Socratic Questioning to dislodge him/her from his "stuck" place. Think of a Goofy Loop as a stuck record. Sometimes you have to nudge the record player a bit to get the record back on track.

Meltdowns

The third intervention point is known as the "Meltdown." A meltdown is defined as a malfunction, and there are three categories of meltdown:

- Physiological meltdown
- Psychological/emotional meltdown
- Technological meltdown

Physiological Meltdown

Physiological meltdowns occur when the student becomes overwhelmed by his/her physiology. Some common examples include his/her heart rate beating out of control, profuse sweating, uncontrollable trembling, temporary paralysis, shortness of breath, or hyperventilation. The best intervention for a physiological meltdown is Socratic Questioning and slowing things down. This is an excellent opportunity to coach your student through Combat Breathing … "In through the nose two, three, four … hold, two, three, four … out through the lips, two, three, four … hold, two, three, four …"

Teaching a stressed-out student how to recognize the onset of a sympathetic nervous system response and how to combat it with Positive Self Talk, Combat Breathing, and replacing fear with anger during a realistic simulation are probably some of the most powerful learning experiences a student will ever be subjected to. In a critical incident in the future, he/she will likely hear your voice and literally take you with him/her into battle. Learn the intervention techniques. They save lives.

Psychological/Emotional Meltdown

The most devastating type of meltdown is the psychological/emotional meltdown. I have seen some students who get shot with NLTA fall down and simulate death. I have seen people get shot with NLTA and flat out quit, throwing their gun on the ground saying "I'm dead." I have seen them go into real psychological trauma, flashing back to real-life situations where they actually faced death. I have seen students void their stomachs or their bladders. I have seen them get a small "owee" and quit. There is no limit to the level of psychological/emotional meltdown that can occur. There will be plenty of time to fix the problem during the remediation, but right there and then you must ensure that he/she gets back into the fight.

Students who are participating in properly structured Reality-Based Training are often experiencing the situation as if it were real … they are in an "altered state" of consciousness (Acosta & Prager, 2002).

A psychological/emotional meltdown can become either a building block or a stumbling stone –the student is malleable clay. Your choice is to mold him/her into something great or pound him/her down into a shapeless mass. As a trainer, you have a moral, and I dare say legal obligation to plant the seeds of greatness, to teach him/her to put the building blocks together, or to shape the clay into an impenetrable wall. This is your opportunity to save a life and to shape future actions.

If a student decides that he/she is "dead" after having been "shot" or "stabbed" during a simulated encounter, that perception has to be immediately fixed. This common problem is the result of a conditioning that was received during a previous negative training or through watching television. If a student makes this self-determination (or actually self-termination) the Exercise Controller needs to perform an intervention, and fast. You must learn to use the Socratic Questioning technique (Carey and Mullan 2004) to help the student develop a solution to the horrible problem he/she is currently facing. Then the student must implement that solution. It cannot be an intellectual exercise ... it must be experiential.

Despite the intervention process described above, the student still has to be remediated so that he/she can experience the situation again and be given the opportunity to use better judgment. It is only through remediation where the student performs successfully that he/she will "own" the experience.

Caught Between a "Rock" and a Hard Place

No trainer is exempt from dealing with unmotivated or difficult students, and I am often asked what to do with the "problem" student ... the person who does not take a personal interest in his own survival, does not take the training seriously, or is otherwise just simply a "rock." This is probably one of the more difficult situations with which an instructor must cope. There is no easy answer to this question, since there is no single explanation for the lackluster performance. Many times, the problem is one of familiarity between the student and the trainer and/or a lack of respect between students and instructors. Sometimes it is a lack of coordination, talent, motivation, lack of job satisfaction, or other physical or emotional problems on the part of the student. Other times it is a result of the instructor being a poor instructor.

No matter what the cause, the short answer is that we cannot give up on these people. It is up to the training staff to provide the best training experience possible. Even if a student is simply "going through the motions," there is no more powerful training medium than experience, and if the quality of the experience is high, it is impossible to not leave some measure of experiential residue on the student at the conclusion of the training session.

Many trainers are hesitant to videotape scenarios because they believe they can be subpoenaed in court to the detriment of the officer and the agency. However, if you are completing the scenarios as I describe (which include a full remediation in the event that performance activities are missed), the video record will demonstrate the student's 100% compliance with policy and public law. Of course there might be places in the video where he/she makes mistakes, but an attorney would rarely be able to take you to task on departmental policy issues if those mistakes are corrected within the training session.

Technological Meltdown

The final type of meltdown that requires an intervention is a technological melt-down. This usually occurs because of a limitation in the training technologies being used. Training weapons are notorious for functional problems, either because of the technical limitations of the technology or operator-induced malfunctions. It is important as an Exercise Controller to have enough experience with the training equipment to know why the technology failed. If it is a problem with the equipment, it must be fixed before re-issuing it to another student.

Another example of shooter error which is often mistakenly attributed to a tech-nological meltdown is chronic malfunctions. Often, this happens when the shooter is "breaking" his/her wrist (limp-wristing) during recoil, resulting in a substantial number of stove-pipe malfunctions. Limp-wristing is not usually enough to induce a malfunction in conventional ammunition, but it will be magnified using the NLTA. Chronic malfunctions with NLTA scream out for the Exercise Controller to watch the student very closely, since there might be some counterproductive things the shooter is doing that might not have been noticeable if they were firing conven-tional ammunition.

There are some chronic malfunctions with NLTA that can be weapon-related. For any of the converted weapons used with popular marking cartridges, it is absolutely essential to use clean firearms that are in good repair, with strong springs and good condition firing pins. Many of the conversion kits are manufactured in such a way as to present the primer slightly off-center to the firing pin. Without strong springs and good quality firing pins, there can be a lot of light primer strikes causing a sig-nificant number of fire malfunctions. Uncleaned guns will result in a lot of feed malfunctions. Using dirty or "shot out" guns for NLTA converted weapons will give you lots of problems.

Regardless of the cause of the malfunction, the important thing is to ensure that the student makes a solid effort to get the weapon back into functional condition and continues the fight. If backup weapons are issued, it will be interesting to see if they will be utilized in the event of a primary weapon malfunction. Watch how officers who are in the habit of carrying backup weapons respond to situations where their primary weapons fail. For those who normally carry a second gun on their ankle for instance, if you do not see them reflexively make an attempt to draw that weapon, even if it is not there because a training version was not issued, it is unlikely that they will go for it in a real life-and-death situation. We will fight as we train, and with the exception of a small majority of tactically minded professionals, very few people in the habit of carrying a secondary weapon train to deploy it in the event that their primary weapon becomes non-functional. A backup weapon often ends up being an afterthought once the action has ended.

The Intervention Questions

The "Rule of Threes" questions for interventions are:

- What are you thinking?
- What is your policy on that?
- From an officer safety perspective, what would be safer?

By blending the science of RBT with the art of Socratic Questioning, we can help a student to emerge from an encounter with a higher level of conditioning where he/she has connected actions with thought, thereby paving the reactive pathways, or torque profiles, which were discussed in Chap. 2.

The question "What are you thinking?" is always the standard question at the beginning of an intervention. I ask, "What are you thinking?" because it is an open-ended question with no pre-conditioning as to what answer is being sought from the student. By asking a student what he/she is thinking, an Exercise Controller will gain some interesting insight on why the student is performing a certain action or saying a certain thing, without interjecting the possibility that he (the instructor) might be making flawed judgments about a student's actions.

By using this questioning technique with the student, the Exercise Controller will help him/her to break any "stuck" pattern that he/she might be experiencing (such as a Goofy Loop) and allow him/her to branch to more effective action.

The Exercise Controller might also find out through asking "What are you thinking?" that the student has no clue as to how he/she is supposed to solve the situation in keeping with policy and safety. This is why the follow-up questions "What is our policy on that?" and "From an officer safety perspective, what is safer?" are so helpful. From a policy perspective, it is essential that an officer be able to articulate before, during, and after an encounter what he/she did and why he/she did it. If you find that he/she is simply functioning without regard to policy and safety, or cannot articulate the correct policy or safety approach, it is time for remedial training and/or classroom instruction.

The exact question "What are you thinking?" is particularly important, and the Exercise Controller must be careful not to use phrases such as "What are you going to do now?" or "Are you going to do anything else?" In the early years during the development of my training programs, I used to ask these other questions. What I discovered is that during Reality-Based Training, regardless of skill level, a student is in a vulnerable setting where at some level he/she is playing the mind game "Guess What the Teacher is Thinking." He/she wants to do well and he/she wants to please the instructor. When I say "What are you going to do now?" or "Are you going to do anything else?" a student often hears, "Do something now" or "Do something else" and he/she might actually take action where he/she probably would not have otherwise. During the debriefing, when I would ask why they acted the way they did, I was often told, "You told me to do something!" Although this was a flawed perception on the part of the student, I discovered that the problem could be avoided by asking, "What are you thinking?" since there was no implication to do something else intrinsic to the question.

Aside from getting students past their stuck points during Goofy Loops and unnatural pauses, the use of the intervention questions is particularly useful during meltdowns because these are the situations where students are the most dejected and are most likely to try to give up. Permitting a student to give up under these circumstances is tantamount to condemning him/her to failure under similar circumstances in the street. As Simon and Acosta pointed out earlier, it is necessary to till this fertile ground and it must be done now, before the brain chemistry can set a pattern of failure. Of all the techniques I teach, intervention is clearly one of the most important behavior altering tools available.

Unnatural Conclusions to a Scenario

The final "Rule of Threes" deals with ending a scenario at the point of an unnatural conclusion, often done for safety reasons. These instances include:

- Safety hazard, immediate or imminent.
- The role player has departed from the script, and it is unclear what is going to happen next.
- The student has taken the scenario in a non-productive direction where no further training value is likely.

Safety Hazards

A safety hazard can be anything from an unauthorized person entering the training area, to protective gear coming off, to a rusty nail sticking out of a board. Under any circumstances where there is a possibility of foreseeable injury, stop the scenario. Let the participants know what is going on, fix the problem if possible (or at the very least, inform the participants of the hazard so it can be avoided), and restart the scenario from the point at which it stopped. No amount of training value that can be garnered from "continuity" is worth the risk of allowing a known safety hazard to go uncorrected.

The Role Player Has Departed from the Script

In the event that a role player has departed from the script, you are in the nebulous world of "anything can happen and it probably won't be good." Use whatever communication tools you have to redirect the role player back to the script if possible.

This is easily accomplished if the role player is equipped with a radio that has a simple earpiece. This gives the Exercise Controller the opportunity to give audible direction to the role player without the student being aware of what is being said. In the absence of radio communication, a set of predetermined hand signals can be used to direct the role player. If all else fails, stop the scenario, approach the role player, and whisper to him/her to get back on track. Give him/her directions on how to respond, then re-start the scenario. A role player who is making up his/her own rules and script is of no value to you, and will often have a distinct negative effect on the training value to the student.

Do not let the scenario control you … you must be in control of the scenario.

The Student Has Taken the Scenario in a Non-productive Direction

There are times when a student goes off on his/her own, using ludicrous tactics or focusing his/her attentions on things that are so far outside the scope of the training, that there is no training value that will likely to come from following him/her down that tortured path.

An agency in the Midwest was doing a scenario involving a vehicle stop where the primary threat was to come from the driver of the vehicle. The scenario was written so that the passenger would bail out and run away from the scene immediately at the beginning of the stop. The trainer wanted to make sure that the student recognized that there was a potential threat from the departed passenger. The scenario began, and after the passenger had bailed out the student began to focus all his/her attention trying to find the departed passenger, leaving the driver in the dust back at the vehicle. The focus of the scenario was gone, and it began to drift without any real training objective.

Situations such as this can often be solved by stepping in, touching the student on the shoulder, and asking the question, "What are you thinking?" The student will likely respond that he/she is concerned about the whereabouts of the passenger. The Exercise Controller can then give the student an "attaboy" by saying, "Good … we wanted to see how you would handle that. What we now know is that another responding unit picked up the passenger a block away. He is in custody. Carry on with the scenario from this point."

If it is appropriate at the conclusion of the scenario, use Socratic Questioning to lead the student to the line of thinking that staying with the vehicle (this is an example for this particular situation, and not a suggestion of a universally accepted tactic) might have been the more appropriate thing to do. Remediate if necessary to ensure all the performance activities have been demonstrated.

This is a basic example, but there are going to be many times when things are going to get out of hand, with the student going off on a tangent. It is important to jump on this as quickly as possible and redirect the focus of the student back to achieving the performance objective.

References

Acosta, J., & Prager, J. S. (2002). *The worst is over: What to say when every moment counts.* Jodere Group.

Booker, B. (2020). *Former Atlanta police officer who shot Rayshard Brooks charged with felony murder.* https://www.npr.org/sections/live-updates-protests-for-racial-justice/2020/06/17/879509659/former-atlanta-police-officer-who-shot-rayshard-brooks-charged-with-felony-murde. Retrieved July 31, 2020.

Carey, T. A., & Mullan, R. J. (2004). What is Socratic questioning? *Psychotherapy: Theory, Research, Practice, Training, 41*(3), 217.

Murray, K. (1995–2020). *Field notes – 1995–2020.*

Thorton, M. (1986). *Miami killers led double lives.* https://www.washingtonpost.com/archive/politics/1986/04/20/miami-killers-led-double-lives/d2ec610f-4e54-4a65-89af-956509698774/. Retrieved July 31, 2020.

Chapter 7
A New Way of Thinking About Training

To begin to see the positive effects of Reality-Based Training at the street level, it is important to understand the underlying psychological architecture of human behavior. The training methods used in a progressive training program must function at both the operative (physical skill) level as well as at the cognitive and pre-cognitive (psychological) level. Trainers must understand the psychology of encounters to dissect and understand the actions of their students so that they can help effect any necessary changes through remedial training.

The scenarios themselves should be simple. In fact, the simpler the better in the early stages, even for seasoned personnel. Just because someone has been on the job for many years, it does not mean he/she will not fail at the basics. Everybody always wants advanced training. Advanced techniques in law enforcement are usually nothing more than the basics done smoother and faster.

Old Training Philosophy

Most of the training that currently occurs takes a backward approach in attempting to achieve its training objectives. The old training philosophy has always been:

- Facility driven

    What can I safely do here?
- Fractured

    Shooting on range
    Fighting in gym
    Thinking in classroom
    No opportunity for "shifting gears"

- Static or linear training environments

© The Author(s), under exclusive licence to Springer Nature Switzerland AG 2021
K. R. Murray, M. R. Haberfeld, *Use of Force Training in Law Enforcement*,
SpringerBriefs in Criminology, https://doi.org/10.1007/978-3-030-59880-8_7

Shooting in one direction
Movement is limited for safety reasons

Much of the training directed toward the development of skills necessary to prevail during lethal force encounters is still being done at the range, using conventional ammunition. Due to the inherently dangerous nature of conventional ammunition, however, in order to assure the physical safety of participants, trainers must be overly concerned with the layout and construction of the training site.

To ensure a safe training environment, training is usually structured so that students are often told what to do rather than taught how to think. Much of this stems from the interest of getting vast numbers of personnel through training programs for the purposes of "qualification" to meet a state-mandated minimum standard. Although it is well-intentioned, it does little to advance the individual skills that the training program had originally been designed to perfect. Officer safety on the street becomes a secondary concern to individual safety on the range. Strangely, these two concerns function at direct odds with each other as many of the behaviors taught at a range are counterproductive to winning or surviving a gunfight. Use of cover, if a consideration at all at the range, often consists of shooting around a four-inch by four-inch post. Shooting positions are usually chosen for the comfort of the shooter and to ensure that students on the firing line are virtually shoulder-to-shoulder so that nobody is forward of anybody else. Strings of fire take on a cadence-like rhythm. Targets face and turn away in predictable intervals and are no longer considered a threat after a prescribed number of hits.

These procedures help reduce injuries at the range, but they condition a set of behaviors that might prove dangerous out in the real world. It is not unusual to see students during a Live Target Engagement (LTE) exercise, standing flat-footed out in the open during a simulated lethal force encounter. Effective use of cover is rarely a consideration for many students. Communication skills are often non-existent. They fire a certain number of shots at the role player regardless of his/her actions, and have been observed re-holstering and relaxing immediately after engaging a suspect, believing that the situation is over. These officers are victims of the conditioning process of the range. They do not clear their malfunctions in a way that would reduce their exposure during a gunfight. They violate the most basic of officer safety guidelines. There is no consideration given to lateral movement, let alone disengagement in the event that they are losing the battle—and they have little or no experience with what to do in the event that they are shot.

New Training Philosophy

The new training philosophy begins with the premise that to be effective, the training must be:

- Performance objective driven.

What are my performance objectives?
What setting would best accomplish that objective?
What training devices will fit the setting?

- That it functions in 360-degree environment, recognizing that there is no better training than *experience*

To begin to build an effective RBT program, it is important to accept that this training must be three-dimensional. Although it may seem like an oversimplification, Captain Joe Robinson tells us that we must remember that in the law enforcement use-of-force model, if an officer chooses to stay engaged with the suspect, there are really only three major categories of things to do to him:

- Talk
- Fight
- Shoot

In scenarios, then, the student must always have access to verbalization options, physical force options, and lethal force.

One of the common mistakes of trainers new to RBT is to arm a student with the only force option the instructor believes will be required to solve the problem as written in the scenario outline; that is, they will give the student a loaded gun and protective gear only if the scenario is a lethal force encounter. Doing this does not provide a trainer an opportunity to test a student's full ability to use his/her judgment, or to observe a student's ability to shift mentally and mechanically between force options. This is a bad habit on the part of trainers that dates back to the days when training was segmented and is an extremely difficult habit for trainers to break.

Some trainers might argue that for scenarios where students are not required to use lethal force, all the protective gear becomes a hindrance to training. The problem with that thinking is that when you provide the protective gear only in the instances where there is an expectation of gunfire, the student is pre-programmed that in the next several minutes something is likely to happen involving a lethal force decision, and he/she is unrealistically keyed up. The most effective RBT programs have the students completely geared up regardless of whether the scenario involves a basic argument that can be resolved through the officer's presence and verbalization options, through a domestic situation that requires some form of intermediate response, to lethal force. When students learn that you are not trying to play the "Gotcha Game," where no matter what they do they will ultimately lose, their responses become much more realistic. This permits trainers to see where a student really needs some training support, rather than observing some artificial response from a student predicated upon what he/she thinks is going to happen.

The Building Blocks of Reality-Based Training

To help design scenarios, I offer six guiding principles or Building Blocks:

1. Define your own reality.

    - Use situations your officers are likely to encounter.
    - Look for patterns of behavior in your agency's case files.
    - Change endings to avoid programmed responses.

2. Set up and enforce strict safety guidelines.

    - If your standard is perfection, your students will be excellent.
    - Unsafe training practices tend to magnify themselves in the real world.
    - Observe and correct all unsafe behaviors.

3. Train within agency policy.

    - Reality-Based Training will bring to light issues for clarification by administration.
    - Play "What if?" in training and fix problems before they occur in real situations.
    - Professionals must have pre-conditioned responses to stressful events.

4. Make training realistic.

    - Use realistic props and training versions of equipment.
    - Use realistic settings.
    - Use realistic situations.

5. Make training stressful.

    - Teach from the simple to the complex to ensure competency.
    - Reality-Based Training requires judgment and teaches situational awareness.
    - Learn to accept and channel the effects of stress.

6. Train officers to win.

    - Do not give it away.
    - Stop "killing" your students in training.
    - The problem with negative reinforcement training.

1. **Define Your Own Reality.**

    - Use situations your officers are likely to encounter.
    - Look for patterns of behavior in your agency's case files.
    - Change endings to avoid programmed responses.

Use Situations Your Officers Are Likely to Encounter

Wasting valuable training time for something that is unlikely to occur happens far too often in scenario training. When you are writing your scenarios, you should:

- Avoid catastrophic events
- Avoid single source experience
- Avoid unrealistic surprises

Catastrophic Events

There is no quick fix for tactical deficiencies in officers. These deficiencies must be fixed one at a time using a building block approach. Reality-Based Training is an effective way of highlighting the areas that need the most attention. Trainers need to observe their officers' deficiencies during simple scenarios, and fix those deficiencies one at a time by connecting proper decision-making with effective action in a stressful setting. This will actually create a neural pathway to successful future responses in similar real-life circumstances. This does not mean that we do not train to overcome those 3% of offenders that Tony Blauer says will actively try to hurt or destroy you. What it means is that fixing the basics and ingraining the necessary skills and mindset to decisively engage a resistive subject will greatly improve the survival likelihood in the event that you find yourself in a catastrophic situation. This is accomplished through basic drills that build in speed and complexity once mastered at the lower levels. Do not try to teach someone how to swim by throwing him/her into a rip tide.

Single Source Experience

It is essential to define the problems that an agency is facing and those that are most likely to cause future trouble. Having a single person write all the scenarios will, unfortunately, present a highly myopic view of those problem areas.

Look for Patterns of Behavior in Your Agency's Case Files

It is not necessary to invent situations when you are developing scenarios, since your own case files likely have plenty of material to draw upon. Statistically, it is the routine situations in which officers are getting injured or poor decisions are being made. Now, if you happen to live in Mayberry and do not have many problems, then look to surrounding jurisdictions for the problems that are occurring there since you can rest assured they are headed your way. National trends, based on the peer-reviewed publications, reputable media source, and FBI statistics are another great place to pull ideas for scenarios.

Change Endings to Avoid Programmed Responses

Having several different endings for a scenario can be useful for several reasons. First, it allows a scenario to branch to different conclusions depending on officer responses. For instance, if an officer performs correctly and limits suspect actions, it might be possible to resolve the problem without violence. However, if the student does not control the suspect's actions, it might result in an escalation to a lethal force encounter.

Changing endings also provides the role player with a little bit of variety to break up the inevitable monotony of doing the same thing over and over. This is useful, since a bored role player has been the cause of many problems that have occurred in Reality-Based Training.

Different endings also permit the challenging of different students at their own skill level. Students who are functioning at a very basic level might be subjected to one set of simple threats, while more advanced students might be subjected to a more complex problem.

Finally, there is the possibility that students might discuss the scenario with others who have not yet been through it. If there are possible alternate endings for the scenarios, this limits a student's ability to come in forewarned as to what the various threat cues might be. Having the possibility for different outcomes makes each student to use his/her own skills to determine the correct type of action.

One difficulty in developing scenarios with multiple endings, however, is that it makes them more difficult to write and to script. As you will see in the next chapter, writing comprehensive scenarios can be quite involved even if there is just one ending! Practice writing single-ending scenarios first, before writing scenarios with complex branches or multiple endings. Simple scenarios can always be expanded once you have the basic format perfected.

2. **Set Up and Enforce Strict Safety Guidelines**

   - If your standard is perfection, your students will be excellent.
   - Unsafe training practices tend to magnify themselves in the real world.
   - Observe and correct all unsafe behaviors.

If Your Standard Is Perfection, Your Students Will Be Excellent

There is a certain freedom associated with having a properly structured scenario and a well-trained, well-scripted role player. Writing scenarios so that you know in advance what the student responses and predictable outcomes should be will liberate an Exercise Controller to focus on the student behaviors. This level of focus permits the observation of the various mechanical and tactical errors that many students will demonstrate during a scenario. Fingers inside trigger guards, struggling or fumbling with pieces of equipment, lack of communication, and disregard for cover are some of the common errors that students make during Reality-Based Training. It is the Exercise Controller's duty to note these problems and bring them to the student's attention at some point during the training session.

The main reason to observe student mistakes and deficiencies is:

Unsafe Training Practices Tend to Magnify Themselves in the Real World

As real as scenarios sometimes seem to a student, they will pale in comparison to an in-his-face life-threatening encounter against an opponent making a concerted effort kill him/her. If unsafe training practices, such as incorrect trigger finger position on a drawn firearm, are not corrected during training, the likelihood is extremely high that in the real-world stress of an armed encounter that finger will continue to be in the wrong place at the wrong time and may lead to a dangerous unintentional discharge.

There is a classic training video, used by some police agencies, of an officer out West who is covering a suspect while another officer is handcuffing him on the ground. The officer on the ground looks up and notices that the cover officer is pointing the weapon dangerously close to him. Seconds later the cover officer has an unintentional discharge into the ground, narrowly missing the suspect.

It is not just sloppy firearms handling that can cause problems. Improper use of radios, batons, TASER®s, chemical agent, or even verbalization can cause problems if not corrected when observed in training.

Therefore, Exercise Controllers must:

Observe and Correct All Unsafe Behavior

When an agency is dragged into court following a use of force, the training that the officer received will invariably come into question. If a student has used questionable techniques or poor judgment in training and the trainer has not corrected those behaviors, it is possible for the student to argue that the agency failed to properly train him/her. Such oversight on the part of the training staff is often unintentional, and the problems would probably have been corrected had they been observed. With the way that scenarios have typically been run, however, this level of observation is rarely possible because there is so much activity occurring during a scenario that a trainer often looks more at the "big picture," rather than analyzing the specific student behaviors, where most of the underlying problems actually reside. Having control of all aspects of a scenario, from proper scenario design through predictable role player behaviors, frees an Exercise Controller to focus his attention almost exclusively on student behaviors.

3. **Train Within Agency Policy**

   • Reality-Based Training will bring to light issues for clarification by the agency.
   • Play "What if?" in training and fix problems before they occur in real situations.
   • Professionals must have pre-conditioned responses to stressful events.

Reality-Based Training Will Bring to Light Issues for Clarification by the Agency

It might seem obvious to say that a trainer should train within agency policy, but they will often unintentionally violate policies in the interest of "flow" within the scenario. For instance, Exercise Controllers have often forced students to continue in a scenario without the resources that they would otherwise have had in a real situation in the interest of preserving the structural integrity of their scenario.

I have observed trainers during a domestic dispute scenario, for example, force an officer to enter a house on his own, telling him/her that there was no backup available. While this is a possibility with some agencies, it was extremely unlikely with this particular agency. The officer expressed reluctance to enter the house alone, indicating that he did not feel safe going in by him/her self and that if it were a real situation he/she would not do it. The Exercise Controller then used that devil of a phrase "Well, for the purposes of this scenario, assume that you have no backup." What followed was a catastrophic event for the student who had to take on two Bad Guys with guns at the same time.

The recommendation is that if a student does something right, such as ask for backup, give him/her an "attaboy," not a spanking. The trainers in the last situation were not interested in providing a survival pathway for their students out of this terrible trap. They wanted to force students into horrific shootings and then orate on the evils of single officer responses to domestic disputes. They were clearly forcing their students to violate officer safety principles as well as departmental policy. This is not training—it is hazing.

Tidying Up Sloppy Departmental Policy

In addition to assuring students understand and function within policy, RBT can be used to clarify departmental policies in situations where they might be a bit muddy, controversial, or in conflict with officer safety principles. And what if there is no policy for a certain situation? This very thing occurred during training with a Midwestern agency, where a scenario had been written in which the clear and correct use of force was lethal force. The student had been on the job for many years, in fact he/she was only a year away from retirement. During the scenario, he/she did not fire at a role player when a clear and present danger requiring lethal force was presented. Following a debriefing and remediation session, the student still refused to shoot.

During an after-action review, the student explained that he/she had made the conscious and moral decision that he/she was unwilling to shoot someone, even if that meant it would cost him/her his/her own life. The immediate problem was to determine what administrative action should be taken against this officer. The agency did not have a policy of removing him/her from street duty, yet if they let him/her back on the street knowing what they knew about his/her refusal to use lethal force, they were in effect endangering the life of the officer, other officers, and the public. This highlighted a gaping policy deficiency for this agency.

This is the type of glaring policy defect that can be brought to light once you have an RBT program in place. It will often highlight specific areas where policy is faulty or non-existent. An effective RBT program can also be used as a vehicle to try to persuade an agency to clean up existing ineffective policies. If you have a policy that is crying out for revision, write a scenario around it, put some people through it, and catalog the results. Present those results to the administration and Risk Management Office and ask for clarification on the departmental policy governing such an occurrence. You will no longer be a "lone voice in the wilderness" asking for clarification, but rather the issue is being raised because it "occurred in training" and you now seek guidance and direction. You may get ignored, but you have created a paper trail which one day might save your career and those of the responding officers' should the policy in question ever lead to a departmental catastrophe. As we all know, catastrophic events always end up with an investigation of the specific actions of the officer and those of the training department.

Play "What If?" in Training and Fix the Problems Before They Occur in Real Situations

The "What if?" game can be used to improve decision-making skills for stressful events. Human beings function much better in situations where they have some level of experience with, even if that experience is simply having thought through a problem. Cataloging decisions intellectually and experientially helps our future decision-making process by integrating previously processed information with experientially integrated information. When it comes to processing information, there are five levels of integration in the human brain and body with which we can concern ourselves. These levels are:

- Data

- Information
- Knowledge
- Understanding
- Conditioning

Understanding is a higher level of integration that corresponds with the level of Conscious Competence, therefore access to that understanding may not be possible in a stressful situation. Because the functioning of the forebrain is substantially curtailed during certain degrees of stress, many repetitions of the desired action are necessary to condition that action to the level of Unconscious Competence to improve the likelihood of adequate performance under stress. There must be a clear neural pathway predicated upon experience to achieve a desired action. Without substantial repetitions or an emotionally significant experience tying the desired response to the stimulating situation, performance of the optimal response is unlikely to occur. If it does occur, it will likely be performed inadequately. This is the reason that:

Professionals Have Pre-conditioned Responses to Stressful Events

If you observe highly skilled combatants in any arena of conflict, you might notice that in the midst of their fierce battle they have an aura of calm about them. This calm emanates from previous conditioning that governs their response to the emerging threat by utilizing the resources and skills that they have honed during training or through previous combat. They have become masters of the terrain of conflict through the conscious management of time, distance, cover, and emotions through confidence in their abilities. This mastery translates into an effective performance in dangerous circumstances.

Make Training Realistic

- Use realistic props and training versions of equipment.
- Use realistic settings.
- Use realistic situations.

Use Realistic Props and Training Versions of Equipment

Muscle memory and proper habits must be developed so that equipment management skills can be taught and tested under stress. This is important for all officers no matter what their skill level is ... from the very inexperienced to the highly advanced. During RBT exercises, it is always fascinating to see some of the bad habits that have been formed during conventional training, and which will ultimately be detrimental in real-life encounters.

Using the actual gear that is going to be used in an operational setting will also permit an astute Exercise Controller to observe the deficiencies that a student might have in working with his/her personal equipment. Functional training versions of personal equipment will clearly demonstrate how well a student will employ them on the street. Will he/she consider wind conditions if he/she chooses to use chemical agent? Will he/she be accurate? Will he/she observe the role player to determine the level of effect? When backup is required, will they actually use the radio and be coherent? Will he/she choose the correct force option or make a grave error such as pulling out his/her TASER® during an encounter that clearly calls for deployment of a lethal option, or the reverse—pulling out his/her pistol when he/she intends to use the TASER®?

While the scenario is in progress, it is important to watch what the student is doing, and also to make some notes to remind yourself during the debriefing to ask him/her about his/her thought processes at certain critical points in the scenario. If you do not make notes about what the student did as the behavior is occurring, you will usually forget to ask about those curious or questionable behaviors, and much of the value of using functional training props to highlight these student deficiencies is lost.

There are various pieces of primary equipment that students will normally carry for which training versions should always be issued no matter what level of force is likely to be used during the scenario. These pieces of equipment include:

- Firearm
- Chemical agent
- Impact weapon
- Handcuffs
- TASER®
- Radio
- Miscellaneous items

Role Player Props

For role players, using realistic props is also essential. A real driver's license with a real name and photo of the role player is one simple example. How many times have you been in a scenario where the role player forgets his/her role player name? Using his/her actual name and having his/her actual driver's license permits the role player to produce actual documents when asked, and it gives him/her less information to remember. This will help the student to focus on the situation and stay "in the scenario" rather than trying to guess what the training staff was thinking when they set up the scenario. Filling baggies with oregano or powdered sugar is better than writing "Simulated Dope" on a piece of cardboard jammed into a pocket. There are lots of cheap and easy ways to create realistic props. The more realistic the situation, the better it is for the student. To that end, if you are a role player, do not wear clothing that says "police" on it. Go to a thrift store and buy a two-dollar jacket.

Casualty simulation will always be difficult, especially given the level of protective equipment that role players must wear. Dummies that have been "bloodied up" make excellent training props for simulated unconscious, severely beaten, or murdered victims. For domestic disturbances or assault situations where a live role player is necessary, it might be necessary to use bloodied rags in combination with descriptive language to fill in some of the blanks for the officer. Having a role player come to the door with a bloodied rag being held to his/her mask and say "that guy beat me in the head with a tire iron … I need to go to the hospital" provides the student with most of the elements he/she needs to arrest the other role player for felony assault. Trying to put makeup on a role player underneath a mask is not effective, and using full-face shields such as riot helmets or laboratory visors so that the face can be seen is dangerous inside a training environment where NLTA is in use. There have already been several serious eye injuries where the visors have flipped up during gun battles and NLTA has struck an unprotected eye.

Use Realistic Settings

State-dependent learning is a term that means "the more realistic the environment a student is training in, the more relevant the experience will be when the mind begins searching for similar experiences during its decision-making phase of problem solving." Just as with the use of realistic training equipment and props, realistic settings free the student to focus on the training situation rather than trying to imagine things that might not actually be there.

For instance, during one of my instructor schools, the training staff had access to a fire tower that they decided would simulate an apartment structure. The scenario involved a suspicious vehicle, and officers were dispatched to investigate it. When the patrol unit approached, a suspect jumped from the car and fired a shot at the officers before he ran into the building.

The correct response according to their departmental policy was to contain the building and call for a special response team. The officers did not do this; instead, they chased the suspect. Rather than stopping the scenario or performing an intervention, the Exercise Controller decided to "see what's going to happen" and permitted the two responding officers to enter the building and begin clearing it on their own.

On the first floor was a substantial amount of clutter that the officers began to clear. The Exercise Controller called a "time out" and told the officers that they were in "the lobby" and they had received an information that the suspect ran up the stairwell. The stairwell was an open stairwell, so one of the officers covered upwards while the other began to clear the stairs. The Exercise Controller again called a "time out" telling the officers to pretend it was a closed stairwell. Frustrated, the officers began to clear the stairwell pretending it was a closed stairwell. The Exercise Controller interrupted again, stating, "For the purposes of this scenario and in the interest of time, you have information that the suspect is on the fifth floor."

On the fifth floor, there was a big open space and two upright pieces of plywood. It was reminiscent of a game show where contestants must decide between door number one and door number two—which one has the prize behind? The officers began to issue challenges, but were interrupted by the Exercise Controller who told them that they first had to simulate a doorway and make entry before they could even "see" the plywood ... it went on and on ...

The point is, although the officers violated a policy to begin with, there was far too much for the officers to have to imagine. This scenario was poorly designed from the beginning. Remember ... when writing a scenario, first pick your problem, and then choose the appropriate setting. If you cannot get a realistic setting for your problem, choose another problem. The more realistic the setting, the better it will be for conditioning proper responses in your students. And since I recommend that training devices must not be selected until after the training setting has been chosen, a realistic setting should be easy to find since many excellent and available training locations are often passed over for use by agencies because they are wedded to the idea that they have to find a site to fit their training devices instead of the other way around. Utilizing the different types of training aids available today, there is no reason why trainers cannot use borrowed structures to provide students with the actual environments they are otherwise looking to simulate. Want to train court deputies? Borrow a courtroom! Need to practice entries in a bank? Borrow a bank! The training sites are available, but you will have to match your training devices to the site to minimize potential damage. Some police trainers have developed excellent relationships with business owners and managers in the community, and have access to any number of buildings for training whenever they want.

Remember the training philosophy hierarchy:

- What are the performance objectives?
- What setting would best accomplish the objective?
- What training devices will fit the setting?

Start with the training objective in mind, find the appropriate setting, and then choose the training devices that would be friendly to that environment. Not all structures or training environments will permit marking versions of NLTA, but not all training scenarios necessitate the use of marking versions of NLTA. I believe that a mixture of available technologies will create the best training program. Choose your devices to fit your setting, not the other way around.

Use Realistic Situations

This sounds so obvious, and yet trainers have a hard time resisting the temptation to let the "silly" factor hijack a perfectly good scenario. "Ninja" role players, silly names for the role players, unlikely occurrences … these all serve to dilute the scenario, and transmit the message to the student that the training is nothing more than "play time." Often, silly scenarios and clownish role player actions are a direct result of training staff boredom, inadequate scenario preparation, lack of training, or lack of experience and confidence on the part of the training staff.

If the scenario retains its realism and professionalism, the student can stay focused on solving the training problem and leaves the session believing in the competence of the staff.

4. **Make Training Stressful**

- Teach from the simple to the complex to ensure competency.
- Reality-Based Training requires judgment and teaches situational awareness.
- Learn to accept and channel the effects of stress.

People do the strangest things under stress, and our animal brains fall back to the laws of primacy and recency; what we learned first, and what we did recently. Actions burned into the brain during stress are difficult to displace, both good and bad.

To understand the power of an emotionally significant event, think about a phobia. Deb Gebeke (1993) notes that beings are born into this world with three innate fears; the fear of sudden motion, loud or abrupt noises, and sudden approach. Everything else is learned.

Phobias result from such powerful one-shot learning experiences that they can handicap a person for life. For example, if you learned to be afraid of bees as a child, it is unnecessary to go back to the hive for "Bee Fear Recurrency Training" at regular intervals. It becomes hardwired into your psyche.

Artwohl (2003), in her Survival Psychology seminars, goes as far as saying that training that does not instill confidence and a sense of mastery is wasted. To build a bank of positive experiences, consider the following:

- Teach from the simple to the complex.
- Teach competency.

- Reality-Based Training requires judgment and teaches situational awareness.
- Learn to accept and channel the effects of stress.

Teach from the Simple to the Complex to Ensure Competency

It is important to start with simple scenarios that test one or two simple choices prior to moving into more complex problems. When catastrophes occur on the street, analysis usually indicates that there was a failure in basic decision-making prior to an officer becoming overwhelmed.

Once the failure chain begins, skills often deteriorate in a vicious downward spiral like the water swirling around the toilet bowl on its way to the sewer. Using very simple scenarios will help officers to understand and condition simple, tactically correct responses to stimuli presented by the suspect. The simpler the decision tree, the quicker the response will be. Siddle (1995), in his book *Sharpening the Warrior's Edge*, refers to Hick's Law. Hick's Law postulates that there is an inverse relationship between the speed of action and the number of choices an officer has to contemplate. When officers have clear and simple choices, their decision loop speeds up. Confidence levels are higher and success is more predictable.

On the other hand, if scenarios are extremely complex or designed as "no win" situations, officers are likely to be overwhelmed and condemned to failure. All of that great brain chemistry is wasted. Well, actually not wasted since it has had its effect. The tragedy is that the effect it has produced is one of conditioning the officer for future failure.

Competency based training requires building a simple decision tree and connecting those simple decisions to specific actions. Because of the way experiences are stored, when they include an emotional component there seems to be a strong pathway back to that torque profile under similar conditions. For effective responses to occur under stress, they must emanate from a programmed dominant response.

During the process of conditioning dominant responses in students, a role player has a key function. To best assist the students in identifying and responding to certain threats it is important to teach role players to initially present threats much more slowly than they would in a real-life situation. Keeping role player actions slow and deliberate permits a student to program a dominant response to such critical incidents. Having successfully responded to a simulated life-threatening experience where the student has been challenged at a stressful but not catastrophic level, he/she will "own" that experience in the future and his/her actions will be faster since his/her situational awareness has improved; his/her OODA loop has been shortened. The speed and efficiency of future actions will improve since skills are being moved from Conscious Competence to Unconscious Competence.

It is essential to build a solid foundation by starting slowly and then improving by building speed. There are many clichés that address this:

- First you get good, then you get fast.

- Speed follows form.
- Perfect practice makes perfect.

Once you have mastered a skill, it is important to do two things. First, there must be some measure of maintenance training done to maintain proficiency. Second, it is important to build on that skill by placing stressors on it in order to improve. That is where advanced training has its place and is how we move from the simple to the complex.

One of the best examples of this teaching principle is the Rogers Shooting School. Bill Rogers has been called the father of modern Reaction Time Shooting. He runs a school that presents steel targets quickly, with the window of opportunity to shoot them closing rapidly. This is not a school to learn basic firearm skills. This is a school to improve relatively well-integrated shooting skills (https://www.rogersshootingschool.com/).

At the Rogers Shooting School, it is virtually impossible to hit the targets if you are grinding your mental gears when you should be shooting. To get faster and hit better, all of the basics of shooting must be improved, and then become wired-in during stressful, timed engagements that require effective threat assessment and good judgment. An inordinate amount of time is spent working on basic skills prior to any of the high-speed tests. After a week of training, most participants can hit quickly and effectively, and they are then simply waiting for the correct stimulus for them to draw and engage the threat targets.

Tony Blauer's Ballistic Micro Fight™ follows a similar principle. Small successes build on each other and combinations of skills are wired together at the psychological and neuro-physiological levels so that when a certain stimulus is received, the correct response is available (Blauer 2020).

The success of both programs speaks for themselves. They are extremely effective models for competency-based skill building. Studies have also shown that the long-term retention of the skills learned in these programs is exceptionally high; often several years. This is obviously due to both the progressive nature as well as the intensity levels of the training.

Many people get frustrated when they are trying to perfect a skill. They achieve a level of proficiency and then seem to hit a "plateau" where there are periods where they do not seem to progress, or sometimes actually regress. George Leonard (1991) describes the learning process as relatively brief spurts of progress, each of which is followed by a slight decline to a plateau somewhat higher in most cases than that which preceded it, and that the plateaus have their own dips and rises along the way. He says that you have to be prepared to spend most of your time on a plateau and keep practicing even when you seem to be getting nowhere.

For any competency-based program to be successful, it must:

1. Start with basic skills and work them until proper form is developed
2. Be progressive so that basic skills that have been perfected are combined into more complex combinations
3. Be realistic so that state-dependent learning can be transferred into similar real-world situations

4. Be relevant so that training time is focused on events that are likely to occur within the job parameters
5. Be comprehensive so that training integrates physical skills with the emotional and cognitive aspects of an encounter

Reality-Based Training Requires Judgment and Teaches Situational Awareness

You cannot teach judgment—only measure it. It is hoped that judgment will improve with experience, but this is not guaranteed. The RBT model allows trainers to observe participants using their judgment to make decisions, and taking actions based on their experience. The desired outcome of RBT is to provide the participant with more experience from which to draw during future encounters.

Situational awareness is a byproduct of experience insofar as it speeds up the internal processing of information. Getting to the "D" of the OODA loop, the "Decision," occurs more rapidly because the observation/orientation aspect has been honed through a situational experience. Using experiential training such as RBT, instructors are able to ascertain the areas where students need additional practice and experience. As F.R. Wilson had pointed out in *Mind, Muscle, and Music,* the brain does not differentiate between good performance and bad performance - it merely catalogs actions in response to stimuli (Wilson 1982).

Therefore, trainers must not attempt to correct poor performance merely by addressing it through verbal critiquing, since this is not likely to translate into improved performance during subsequent encounters. Poor performance must be corrected experientially otherwise the only experience a student will have will be that of his/her sub-optimal performance, that is, he/she will be basing his/her future performance on his/her past failures. This is the importance of immediate remediation and why it is so essential to the programming of an optimum response. By connecting the cognitive component of "what should be done" with the physical response of "what will be done," judgment and situational awareness have shown vast improvement over the previously used negative training models.

It is important to note that there is a "window of opportunity" for correcting the behaviors before the negative experience "gels" in the subconscious mind. Typically, much of the integration will occur during the next sleep cycle. Remediation must not be left undone or even postponed until the following training session.

The last words of this chapter belong to one of the co-authors, Haberfeld (2018) who advocates strongly for what she refers is as "proactive training" as opposed to a "dilletante-reactive" approach to training, as exhibited by most of the police departments, in the aftermath of a high profile event and scandals. Reforms to police training should be a function of innovations in research and technology and not an afterthought following a scandalous event and this should be the "new way" of thinking about police training.

References

Artwohl, A. (2003). No recall of weapon discharge. *Law Enforcement Executive Forum, 3*(2), 41–49.

Blauer, T. (2020). *High gear*. Retrieved July 25, 2020. https://blauerspear.com/whyhighgear

Gebeke, D. (1993). *Children and fear*. North Dakota State University. Retrieved January 21, 2009. http://www.ag.ndsu.edu/pubs/yf/famsci/he458w.htm

Haberfeld, M. R. (2018). *Critical issues in police training*. Boston: Pearson Custom Publishing.

Leonard, G. B. (1991). *Mastery: The keys to long-term success and fulfillment*. New York: Dutton.

Murray, K. (1995–2020). *Field notes*. Rogers Shooting School. (2020). Retrieved July 25, 2020. https://www.rogersshootingschool.com/

Siddle, B. K. (1995). *Sharpening the Warrior's edge*. Millstadt: PPCT Research Publications.

Wilson, F. R. (1982). Mind, muscle and music. *American Music Teacher, 32*(1), 12–15.

Chapter 8
Conclusion and Final Thoughts

Debrief, Remediation, and After Action Review

At the end of the training exercise, a debriefing and any necessary remediation is essential. The military has for a long time understood the value in mission debriefing and remediation.

Many current training scenarios take the following form:

- Student arrives on the scene
- Student gets hit/shot/stabbed/blown up/etc.
- Exercise Controller stops the scenario and declares the student "dead"
- Exercise Controller orates on what the student did wrong
- Exercise Controller asks if there are any questions
- Student leaves the training having experienced being "killed," and quite possibly thinking that the training is stupid

Until a more effective way to run scenarios and debriefings was developed, this was the predominant model for scenario implementation and debriefings. Some trainers still use this model for training and are often frustrated when the student makes mistakes on things that he/she should "know" better.

If you have been, or will be, involved in an RBT, you too will observe students do the strangest things. The crux of the problem is that although the student knows better, he/she is suffering from a lack of experience.

There are four steps that can be used to guide the student to higher learning during the Reality-Based Training process.

These steps are:

- The scenario
- The debriefing
- The immediate remediation
- The after action review

© The Author(s), under exclusive licence to Springer Nature Switzerland AG 2021 97
K. R. Murray, M. R. Haberfeld, *Use of Force Training in Law Enforcement*,
SpringerBriefs in Criminology, https://doi.org/10.1007/978-3-030-59880-8_8

Scenario

The scenario itself has been thoroughly covered, so there is nothing further to add at this point. The debriefing occurs immediately following the conclusion of the scenario.

Debriefing

The debriefing is defined as a full recap and walk-through of what happened during the scenario. It should take the form of a "question and answer" session between the Exercise Controller and the student, with the student explaining his/her thoughts and actions to the Exercise Controller as if the Exercise Controller was not present during the event. It takes some measure of practice to perfect this technique, but it is an extremely valuable teaching tool. Anyone with investigative experience will have an advantage in doing this quality of "walk-through" since the debriefing should proceed as if the Exercise Controller was not actually there to see the entire event.

At the conclusion of the scenario, the Exercise Controller should use the Socratic Questioning approach to guide the student through a debriefing, resisting the temptation to orate, or "tell" the student what he (the Exercise Controller) observed. On the clipboards that are issued to the Exercise Controllers in my five-day instructor schools, the words "Ask, Don't Tell" are emblazoned at the top of their Cheat Sheet. This prompts the Exercise Controller to ask a question, then shut up and listen to the answer. You will be amazed what you can learn from a student regarding his/her behaviors using this technique. For the most part, it is also non-threatening, which means the student is more likely to open up to you, rather than try to justify his/her lackluster performance. I say "for the most part" because at some point you will switch from "investigator" to "prosecutor."

The most effective way to begin the debriefing is with the standard phrase "So ... walk me through what just happened ... what did we have?" The goal is to get the student to begin describing the situation from the beginning. As the debriefing continues, the Exercise Controller asks higher-level questions about the critical portions of the scenario. When students are first exposed to this quality of training process and they are asked to describe what happened, their tendency is to jump right into the description of the "action" part. Slow them down. Remember, we are less interested in the final answer as we are in the whole equation. Bring them back to the beginning, both mentally and physically. For instance, if they started out in their vehicle, take them back to their vehicle. Start by using the phrase "Let's start at the beginning ... what kind of call did you have?" Then take the student step-by-step through the scenario while looking at the Evaluation Sheet for any notes that were made to jog your memory about questions relating to student behaviors.

There will be points during the debriefing where the student either handled things well or performed in a less-than-optimal manner. When these points are reached, ask something to the effect of "And when that happened, what did the role player do?" The student will respond, and the Exercise Controller continues … "And how did you respond?" This is usually the point where the student either did or did not perform correctly. If the student responded correctly, give him/her an "attaboy" … "Yeah … I really liked what you did there … you did great … then what happened?"

If he had responded incorrectly, refer back to the role player's actions that followed after the student's inappropriate response, and tie the incorrect action to the consequential actions of the role player. For example, if a student should have separated two arguing brothers yet he did not, and the brothers started fighting again, you could ask "What's our policy on that?" When the student replies that he should have physically separated the brothers, ask "And what happened when you allowed the brothers to stay close together or in the same room?" and have him/her describe the consequences of improper action.

Avoid questions that deal with "feelings," such as when the student describes one of the actions that they took against a role player. Do not use questions like "How did you feel about what you did?" It is unimportant how the student "feels" about their actions. All that is important is whether the actions were appropriate and sufficient. To that end, it is better to ask questions like "What did you do?" then "What effect did that have on the suspect?" and then, "Is there something else that you might have done that could have been more effective?" These types of questions deal with cause and effect and will lead to more effective action in the future.

The process as described above may sound a bit confusing, but there is a sample dialogue toward the end of this section that gives you a better idea of the flow of a debriefing, including how to utilize various questions to both ensure that a student can justify any force that he/she has used, as well as suggestions on how to teach a student to tighten up his/her explanations.

It is essential that a student be able to justify his/her actions following any use of force, and he/she should be able to justify them with conviction since, in the real world, he/she must be able to do so in court. Remember, surviving critical incidents is not just a physical event … professional survival is also at stake.

To condition your students to survive professionally, it is helpful to change the tone of your questioning during the debriefing while discussing any use-of-force event. During most of the walk-through, the tone of questioning is rather casual, and questions that help a student recall the details are employed. At the point where the student begins describing his/her use of force, the tone of questioning should become more prosecutorial.

For example, if a student states that he/she "… shot the suspect …" one of the questions I often use is, "Yeah … (pause … switch tone from investigator to prosecutor) … what did you do that for?" with an intonation that would rival a parent asking a child why he/she scribbled on the wall with a magic marker. This will often take the student off guard and cause him/her to become defensive. This is a natural response to being attacked, and the goal of utilizing this type of debriefing technique is to help him/her learn to overcome his/her defensive responses. This is a useful skill when dealing with hostile attorneys who will be grilling him/her about his/her actions, or when answering questions from his/her superiors or other investigators during a subsequent review of an incident.

Immediate Remediation

Immediate remediation is the concept that is used to take the fertile soil that I spoke of earlier, and plant those seeds of greatness. One form of immediate remediation occurs during the scenario at a point where a student becomes "stuck." As described during the section on interventions, a student will often change his/her actions following an intervention. This is a much more subtle form of remediation although it may not absolve the student of having to repeat the scenario, or a part of the scenario, at the conclusion of the debriefing to ensure that each of the performance activities is accomplished.

There are people in the training community who would say that it is necessary to completely change the scenario during a remediation, arguing that it is important that the student does not "know" the outcome so that he/she will respond to what he/she is seeing rather than what he/she already knows. The problem here is that the officer does not yet "own" the experience. Well-intentioned (but untrained) Exercise Controllers and role players tend change things during the remediation. This causes a "jangle" effect on the student's neurological librarian—the survival experience has not been properly "filed" yet, and changing behaviors solely for the purpose of "surprising" the student often does more harm than good.

Using the remediation model creates powerful change in students. It admittedly takes longer than the old oration method, but it provides a meaningful learning experience as well as a conditioned response to a life-threatening event. Although an effective debriefing can take quite a bit of time, the remediation itself is likely to go rather quickly and much more smoothly than the original run-through, but it is absolutely necessary for the student to "own" the experience.

Forcing each student to complete the scenario and winning the initial encounter through perseverance or tactical superiority creates a winning mind. Remediating the experience so that the officer utilizes the proper force for a given situation and making sure he/she continues until the situation reaches its natural conclusion programs an effective dominant response to various threat cues. Ultimately, the goal is to catalyze an uncompromising belief system that there is no possibility of losing, so that the student will never give up during a hostile encounter.

After Action Review

This is a bit of a luxury, but it adds a deeper degree of learning if there is sufficient time. An after action review is defined as a broad discussion of the training event utilizing peer review, subject matter experts, and data. Once a group of students has experienced a particular scenario, it is helpful to get that group together and discuss the common successes and failings that many of the students had experienced. This does not only reinforce the valuable skills that have been integrated, but also help diffuse any feelings of inadequacy that might be left over.

During an after action review, it is useful to show a video recording of the scenarios. The instructor must not focus on individual failings, but instead group commonly demonstrated errors together, using language such as:

- Notice the tendency of many officers to stand out in the open while they are shooting.
- Do you see how many officers are exposed despite the fact they think they are behind cover?

It is permissible to use individual examples of excellent technique as long as you do not continually use the same person as the "star" since this can polarize the group and create unnecessary animosity or professional jealousies between the participants. After reviewing the videos recorded during the training, a video footage of others who experienced similar problems in real life (such as dashcam or amateur videos) helps make the point that the scenario they just experienced can really happen "out there." There are many sources for these video clips, especially where shootings are involved.

The use of subject matter experts can also be extremely helpful during an after action review since they can provide an academic and experiential knowledge base for justification of the force options that have been used throughout the training.

During an after action review, when a student discovers that others made the same mistakes that he/she did, it makes his/her own errors more tolerable. And when, as a group, their skills have all improved compared with when they first arrived for training, a kinship is formed. Bonds forged in the fires of combat, even simulated combat, help to make everyone work closer together out in the real world.

From the perspective of winding down after a hard day of training, students also love to see themselves on video, so it is a nice, relaxed way to end the day. If you do not have the time, a lesser form of an after action review that I call reflective review is also helpful. You can provide the student with a copy of his/her video and a short written piece on the policy and law that covers their performance objectives. Students will then could review their own performance.

Final Thoughts

Reality-Based Training is a complicated undertaking, and to believe that you can jump right into it by purchasing some equipment and taking a day or two to sketch out a few scenarios is exactly how most agencies begin, and ultimately why accidents or poor quality training occurs. If you are feeling overwhelmed at this point by the amount of planning, coordination, and effort that will be required to build an optimum training program, good! It is not supposed to be easy. The fact that you are feeling overwhelmed means that you have been paying attention, and that is the very first step toward developing an excellent program that will really make a difference to your officers specifically, your agency in general, and your community as a whole.

If you are at the beginning stages of an RBT program, accept the fact that it will take time to build your program. Expect to invest several years in trying to get your program going to the point where people inside your agency begin to support you in your efforts. There are no overnight successes in this business, and that is even if you do everything right! But there can certainly be instantaneous disasters if you do one or two particular things wrong. Take the time necessary to build in the safeguards that will ensure you are planting the seeds of greatness, so that your program becomes a successful legacy which will be left to those who will come after you.

A student needs to "learn how to learn" and also to trust that the RBT exercise is designed to teach him/her how to win in difficult encounters. To that end, he/she must have the courage to fail, knowing that when he/she stumbles, a competent instructor is there to observe and analyze his/her shortcomings, and provide him/her an immediate path to success. In a supportive environment such as this, over time students will begin coming to training with no preconceptions about what will happen during the scenario, except that they will be secured in the knowledge that their judgment and skills will improve as a result of the training. They will then simply perform based on their training and experience. They will demonstrate realistic responses to realistic stimuli, knowing that there will be an opportunity to correct any substandard behavior and emerge from the scenario as a winner.

We would be remiss not to mention some important empirical research findings, published in the past few years, that point to the correlation between use of force, procedural justice, racial biases, traditional police culture (Lee et al. 2010; Mears et al. 2017; Rahtz 2003; Rajakaruna et al. 2017; Rojek et al. 2012, Silver et al. 2017; Staller and Zaiser 2015; Wolfe et al. 2020), and effective police training. This brief does not claim to be the panacea for the current deficiencies in the training of use of force, instead it proposes a more tactical/experiential contour or template to be considered by the ones responsible for police training.

References

Lee, H., Jang, H., Yun, I., Lim, H., & Tushaus, D. W. (2010). An examination of police use of force utilizing police training and neighborhood contextual factors. *Policing: An International Journal of Police Strategies & Management, 33*(4), 681–702.

Mears, D. P., Craig, M. O., Stewart, E. A., & Warren, P. Y. (2017). Thinking fast, not slow: How cognitive biases may contribute to racial disparities in the use of force in police citizen encounters. *Journal of Criminal Justice, 53*, 12–24. https://doi.org/10.1016/j.jcrimjus.2017.09.001.

Rahtz, H. (2003). *Understanding police use of force*. Monsey: Criminal Justice Press.

Rajakaruna, N., Henry, P. J., Cutler, A., & Fairman, G. (2017). Ensuring the validity of police use of force training. *Police Practice and Research, 18*(5), 507–521.

Rojek, J., Alpert, G. P., & Smith, H. P. (2012). Examining officer and citizen accounts of police use-of-force incidents. *Crime & Delinquency, 58*(2), 301–327. https://doi.org/10.1177/0011128710386206.

Silver, J. R., Roche, S. P., Bilach, T. J., & Ryon, S. B. (2017). Traditional police culture, use of force, and procedural justice: Investigating individual, organizational, and contextual factors. *Justice Quarterly, 34*(7), 1272–1309. https://doi.org/10.1080/07418825.2017.1381756.

Staller, M. S., & Zaiser, B. (2015). Developing problem solvers: New perspectives on pedagogical practices in police use of force training. *The Journal of Law Enforcement, 4*(3), 1–15.

Wolfe, S., Rojek, J., McLean, K., & Alpert, G. (2020). Social interaction training to reduce police use of force. *The Annals of the American Academy of Political and Social Science, 687*(1), 124–145.

Index

A
Accidental shooting, 50, 52
The Ace Factor, 37
Active shooter training, 45
Adequacy, 9
Administrative actions, 38
After action review, 97, 100, 101
Agency, 83
AirSoft pistols, 56
American Psychiatric Association, 20
Anticipation mindset, 42
Anti-socialization factors, 26
Anxiety, 15
Articulable, 28

B
Ballistic Micro-Fight™, 29
Battle fatigue, 20
Behavioral realities, 47
Blauer's comprehensive program, 28, 29
Blauer's S.P.E.A.R. SYSTEM techniques, 15
Blauer's TCMS, 29
Bloodstream, 14
Body worn cameras (BWC), 3, 4
Boyd's Loop, 29
Brain processes, 13
Breath and shaky muscles, 18
Building basic skills, 59
Building blocks, 81, 83

C
Casualty simulation, 90
Catch-22, 25
Changing endings, 84

Chronic malfunctions, 73
Citizen-complaints *vs.* police, 3
Classic training video, 85
Coearcive force, 2
Cognitive processing, 21
Communication skills, 80
Communication tools, 75
Community-Oriented Policing, 1
Competency-based program, 94
Competency-based skill building, 94
Competency based training, 93
Complacent mindset, 42
Conditioning dominant responses, 93
Confrontation, 29
Confrontational simulation (Con-Sim), 49
Conscious Competence (CC), 10, 11,
      49–76, 88, 93
Conscious Competence of Unconscious
      Competence, 10
Conscious incompetence, 10
Conscious mind, 11
Conscious resources, 11
Conventional paintball guns, 56
Creating a survival sentence, 12
Crimes in progress, 42
Criminal element, 25
Criminal justice system, 1
Crisis Intervention Training (CIT), 32
Critical encounter, 30

D
Dash cams, 47
Deadly force, 41
Deadly Force Encounters (book), 20
Death decisions, 7

© The Author(s), under exclusive licence to Springer Nature Switzerland AG 2021   105
K. R. Murray, M. R. Haberfeld, *Use of Force Training in Law Enforcement*,
SpringerBriefs in Criminology, https://doi.org/10.1007/978-3-030-59880-8

Debriefing, 97
    definition, 98
    effective debriefing, 100
    goal, 98
    RBT process, 97
    and remediation, 97, 100
    role player's actions, 99
    scenario implementation, 97, 98
    Socratic Questioning approach, 98
    use of force, 99
Decision-making process, 30
Decision processes, 34
Decisive factors, 30
De-escalation, 8, 27, 28
Defining reality, 82
Deliberate lethal force, 33, 34
Departmental policies, 86
Disengagement, 28
Domestic dispute scenario, 86
Dominant response, 20–21
DRAW, 12
Duty deaths, 42

E
Effective RBT program, 81, 87
Electronic devices, 3
Emergency service workers, 21
Emotional Climate Drill™, 28
Emotional Motion Drill™, 29
Enabling process, 25
ENGAGE, 13
Errors of judgment, 3
Escalation, 8, 28
Exercise controller, 32
Experiential training, 49, 72
Extraordinary measures, 31
Eye/hand coordination skills, 14

F
Fear, 15
Field problems, 49
Fighting, 22, 23
Firearms training
    acquisition, 9
    CC, 10, 11
    conscious incompetence, 10
    NLP, 10
    scoring system, 9
    UC, 11–13
    unconscious incompetence, 10
Force-on-force training program, 49, 53, 56

Force skills, 41
Full-contact practice fights, 43

G
Gaining submission, 29
Genetic coding, 2, 38
Goofy Loop, 69, 70, 74, 75
"Gotcha Game", 81
Gun, 12

H
Handicap, 3
Heart rate, 18, 19
Hesitation, 38, 39
High-quality simulation training, 32
Hiring practices, 45
Human body, 14
Human Diversity Refresher training, 50
Human factors, 3

I
Identical equipment manipulation, 58
Immediacy of threat, 30
Immediate remediation, 97, 100
Immediate vs. imminent, 34–35
Incapacitating physical interventions, 27
In-policy shooting, 34
Intellectual exercise, 72
Internal administrative pressure, 7
Interval training, 11
Intervention points, 69
Interventions, 68, 69, 74
Intuition, 42
Inverted "U" hypothesis, 18
Investigative functions, 42

J
Jangle effect, 21, 100

K
Kill-houses, 38
Killing Enabling Factors, 26
Killing experience, 25, 26

L
Law enforcement, 7, 8, 79
    force, 45

hiring practices, 45
   killing experience, 41
Legal updates, 50
Lethal encounters, 2, 3
Lethal force, 25, 26, 80, 81, 87
   deliberate, 33, 34
   justification *vs.* necessity, 31–33
   reactive, 33, 34
   spontaneous, 33, 34
Level of customer service, 28
Life-threatening encounter, 14
Live Action Response Drill™, 29
Live Target Engagement (LTE) exercise, 52,
      53, 55, 56, 80
Ludicrous tactics, 76

M
Martial arts, 2
May-Shoot scenarios, 34
Mechanics of conflict, 29
Media coverage, 44
Meltdown
   definition, 70
   emotional, 71
   physiological, 71
   technological, 71, 73
Memphis Model, 32
Military training, 41
Mock disasters, 49
Muscle memory, 12, 89

N
Natural conclusion, 63–65
Negative reinforcement training, 46
Negative self-talk, 21
Negative training experiences, 43, 46
Neuro-Linguistic Programming (NLP), 10
Neurological effects, 21–23
New training philosophy, 80, 81
"Ninja" role players, 92
Non-aggressive intervention, 44
Non-Lethal Training Ammunition (NLTA), 53,
      56–58, 71, 73

O
Officer safety, 80, 86
Old training philosophy, 79, 80
On Killing (book), 3
OODA concept, 29
Op-for training, 49

Optimal performance zone, 18
Out-of-policy shooting, 34

P
Pain penalties, 53–57
Pattern of constitutional violations, 33
Patterned breathing, 19
Perception of threat, 27, 30, 33, 34
Perceptual distortion, 19, 20
Perceptual memory distortions, 20
Permanent disfigurement, 53
Personal equipment, 89
Physical confrontation, 66, 67
Physical skills, 8
Physical training, 8
Physiological impairments, 18
Physiological meltdowns, 71
Physiological memory, 12
Physiology of stress, 18
Police-citizen encounters, 4
Police performance, 18, 20
Police retraining, 45
Police training, 1–4
Poor performance, 95
Poor tactics, 46, 47
Post-traumatic stress disorder
      (PTSD), 20, 26
Posturing, 23, 30
Practice transitional techniques, 8
Pre-conditioning, 2
Predisposition of the Killer, 26
Proactive trainers, 36
"Professional switch", 42
Profiling, 2
Program effectiveness, 7
Projectile-based training, 53, 57
Protracted negotiations, 30
Psychological barriers, 8, 9
Psychological/emotional
      meltdown, 71, 72
Psychological evaluations, 26
Psychological factors, 3
Psychological scales, 41
Psychology of training, 8
Public safety, 2
Punishment, 46

Q
Qualification, 45
Questionable media practices, 44
Quick life, 7

R
Range training, 68
RBT exercises, 89, 102
Reactive, 37, 38
Reactive lethal force, 33, 34
Realism, 43
Realistic setting, 90, 91
Realistic training, 88
Reality-based comprehensive training
    system, 8
Reality-based firearms, 8
Reality-based training (RBT), 1, 3, 28, 36,
        38, 42, 46
    accidental shooting, 52
    agencies, 52
    ammunition, 51
    block training, 50
    building blocks, 81, 82
    defining reality, 82
    equipment and ammunition, 51
    eye/hand coordination, 14
    fear, 15
    firearms (*see* Firearms training)
    force-on-force, 56
    hurting people, 52
    judgment and situational awareness, 95
    LTE, 52, 53, 55, 56
    NLTA, 53, 57
    officer's ability, 59
    on-duty/in-service training, 50
    psychological barriers, 8, 9
    questioning technique, 74
    Socratic Questioning, 74
    at street level, 79
    stress, 14, 15
    training methods, 79
Real-life videos, 47
Reasonable Doubt, 2
Reloading techniques, 58
The Reluctant Warrior, 7, 8
Remediation
    and debriefing, 97
    immediate remediation, 97, 100
    "jangle" effect, 100
    in students, 100
Role play, 66
Role players, 90
"Rule Of Threes" questions, 74
Rules of engagement
    and force policy
        Blauer's comprehensive
            program, 28, 29
        continued application, 28

    de-escalation, 28
    disengagement, 28
    escalation, 28
    experiential model, 28
    explanation dealing, 31
    gaining submission, 29
    hiding/stalling, 30
    incapacitating physical
        interventions, 27
    mistaken impression, 27
    OODA concept, 29
    RBT, 28
    rules of holes, 27
    single method, 27
    teaching, 31
    tools and techniques, 27
    and guidelines, 25
    hesitation, 38, 39
    immediate *vs.* imminent, 34–35
    killing experience, 26
    lethal force (*see* Lethal force)
    reactive, 37, 38
    sensitivity retraining, 26, 27
    unclear force policies, 35, 36
Rules of holes, 27

S
Safe training environment, 80
Safety, 43
Safety guidelines, 80, 82, 84
Safety hazard, 75
Scenario training, 46, 47, 82
    critical/life-threatening situations, 64
    Exercise Controller, 60, 61
    high-level, 59
    intervention points, 69
    natural conclusions, 63–65
    safety reasons, 63
Self-deprecating beliefs, 21
Self-destructive offenders, 32
Self-discipline, 8
Self-mastery, 8
Sensitivity retraining, 26, 27
SGI (Silicon Graphics), 37
Shoot-houses, 38
Shooting skills, 11
Simulated gunfire, 62, 68
Simulation program, 50
Simulation-training program, 3
Situational awareness, 82, 92, 93, 95
Skill, 9
Skill mastery, 9

"Smart Gun", 45
Social environment, 2
Social media, 44
Socialization factors, 25, 26
Socratic Questioning, 70–72, 74, 76, 98
Specialized training, 45
Spontaneous lethal force, 33, 34
Startle-flinch response, 15
State-dependent learning, 90, 95
Stress, 9, 14, 15, 58–60
    inoculation, 37, 59
    neurological effects, 21–23
    recognition, 17
Student behaviors, 85, 86
Suicide by cop, 32
Survival Scores Research Project, 18
Survival sentence, 12
SWAT mission, 44
Sympathetic media coverage, 44
Sympathetic nervous system, 14, 15,
        21, 55, 71
Systematic breathing, 19

T
Tactical Confrontation Management System
        (TCMS), 28
Tactical decisions, 8, 13
Tactical situations, 42, 44, 46
TASER®, 89
Technological meltdown, 71, 73
Torque profile, 13
Training
    exercise, debriefing, 97
    fragmentation, 46
    law enforcement, 7
    life experience, 44
    methods, 7
    programs, 9
    safety and realism, 43
    scenarios, 97, 98
    simulations, 9, 33
    technologies, 55, 57

U
Unclear force policies, 35, 36
Unconscious Competence (UC), 11–13, 21,
        55, 58, 88, 93
Unconscious incompetence, 10
Understanding, 88
Unnatural conclusions, 63, 75
Unnatural pauses, 69, 70, 75
Unprovoked attacks, 42
Unrealistic beliefs
    dominant response, 20–21
    heart rate, 18, 19
    neurological effects of stress, 21–23
    perceptual distortion, 19, 20
    stress recognition, 17
    visual narrowing, 19
Unsafe training, 82, 84, 85
Use-of-force incidents, 3
Use-of-force policies, 25
Use-of-force simulation training, 49, 51, 65
Use-of-force teaching, 46

V
Vehicle stops, 42
Verbal communication, 30
Video simulators, 68
Violent encounter, 7
Visual narrowing, 19

W
*Wet Mind - The New Cognitive
        Neuroscience*, 13
"What if?" game, 87–88
Window of opportunity, 94, 95
Writing scenarios, 84

Y
Youth violence, 45

Printed in Great Britain
by Amazon